Multicultural Horizons

Multiculturalism is and always has been a deeply emotive and highly contested issue. The intensity of feelings that multiculturalism invariably ignites is considered in this timely analysis of how the 'New Britain' of the 21st century is variously re-imagined as multicultural. Introducing the concept of 'multicultural intimacies', Anne-Marie Fortier offers a new form of critical engagement with the cultural politics of multiculturalism, one that attends to ideals of mixing, loving thy neighbour and feelings for the nation. In the first study of its kind, Fortier considers the anxieties, desires, and issues that form discourses of 'multicultural Britain' available in the British public domain. She investigates:

- the significance of gender, sex, generations and kinship, as well as race and ethnicity, in debates about cultural difference;
- the consolidation of religion as a marker of absolute difference;
- 'moral racism', the criteria for good citizenship and the limits of civility.

This book presents a unique analysis of multiculturalism that draws on insights from critical race studies, feminist and queer studies, post-colonialism, and psychoanalysis. The book will appeal to undergraduates, postgraduates and researchers interested in the cultural politics of neo-liberal ideals of diversity management, tolerance, and the national fantasy.

Anne-Marie Fortier is Senior Lecturer in Sociology at Lancaster University. Her research interests revolve around critical race studies, critical migration studies, feminist, queer and post-colonial theory. She is the author of *Migrant Belongings* (2000) and co-editor of *Uprootings/Regroundings* (2003).

International Library of Sociology

Founded by Karl Mannheim
Editor: John Urry
Lancaster University

Recent publications in this series include:

Theories of the Information
Society, 3rd Edition
Frank Webster

Mediating Nature
Nils Lindahl Elliot

Haunting the Knowledge Economy
*Jane Kenway, Elizabeth Bullen,
Johannah Fahey, and Simon Robb*

Global Nomads
Techno and new age as
transnational countercultures in
Ibiza and Goa
Anthony D'Andrea

The Cinematic Tourist
Explorations in globalization,
culture and resistance
Rodanthi Tzanelli

Non-Representational Theory
Space, politics, affect
Nigel Thrift

Urban Fears and Global Terrors
Citizenship, multicultures and
belongings after 7/7
Victor J. Seidler

Sociology Through the Projector
*Bülent Diken and Carsten Bagge
Laustsen*

Multicultural Horizons
Diversity and the limits of the civil
nation
Anne-Marie Fortier

Multicultural Horizons

Diversity and the limits of the civil nation

Anne-Marie Fortier

Routledge
Taylor & Francis Group

LONDON AND NEW YORK

First published 2008
by Routledge
2 Park Square, Milton Park, Abingdon, Oxon OX14 4RN

Simultaneously published in the USA and Canada
by Routledge
270 Madison Avenue, New York, NY 10016

Routledge is an imprint of the Taylor & Francis Group, an informa business

© 2008 Anne-Marie Fortier

Typeset in Sabon by
Taylor & Francis Books
Printed and bound in Great Britain by
TJ International Ltd, Padstow

British Library Cataloguing in Publication Data
A catalogue record for this book is available from the British Library

Library of Congress Cataloging in Publication Data
ISBN 978-0-415-39608-0 (hard cover) – ISBN 978-0-415-39607-3
(paper cover) 1. Great Britain–Ethnic relations. 2. Multiculturalism–
Great Britain. 3. Great Britain–Race relations. 4. Minorities–Great
Britain. I. Title.
DA125.A1F67 2007
305.800941–dc22
2007020167

ISBN13: 978-0-415-39608-0 (hbk)
ISBN13: 978-0-415-39607-3 (pbk)

Contents

Acknowledgments

The idea for this project was conceived in 2000, when former Tory Leader William Hague declared 'we are a nation of immigrants' in the context of a pubic debate over the 'Parekh Report' on the future of multi-ethnic Britain (see Chapter 2). What struck me was that Hague was not alone in re-writing the national as multicultural; as shown in Chapter 2, there was a quasi-consensus at the time that Britain was and always has been inher-ently multicultural. Moreover, New Labour, especially former Prime Min-ister Tony Blair, was trumpeting diversity and the 'multicultural' as a defining feature of its vision for the 'new Britain' of the 21st century. I was hooked. What is the role of the 'new' as a way of rewriting history and of redefining Britishness? As a French-Canadian Québécoise who had been living in Britain for almost 15 years, Hague's and Blair's statements, and the statements of others, seemed to me both extraordinary and banal. Extraordinary because it seemed like a rewriting of the British nation, a revisiting of British history as constituted through a timeless *im*migration, and as if Hague (and countless others) was redefining the national 'original folk' as immigrants. At the same time, the statement appeared to me to be utterly banal in its resonance with the mantra that I grew up with in Canada, a white settler society self-defined as a 'nation of immigrants'. But for all the resonances that the phrase sounded in my mind, what intrigued me was: what *is* the British version of multiculturalism? What are the spe-cificities of the current British historical conjuncture that necessitates *this* (or these) version(s) of multiculturalism? What anxieties, desires, dreams, and nightmares are mobilized in the utopian or dystopian horizons of 'multicultural Britain'? From then on – from 2000 to 2006 – multi-culturalism was to make regular headlines in the British national press, and be the subject of intense political and public debate. Though this book is not about Blair government policies *per se*, it covers the circulation and contested definition of 'multicultural Britain' during the Blair era.

In the course of writing this book, I benefited from numerous conversa-tions with colleagues and friends who have each helped me in thinking through some of the issues addressed here. Thanks to Sara Ahmed, Les Back, Lauren Berlant, Anick Druelle, Paul Fletcher, Jessica Higgs, Peter

Hopkins, Danielle Juteau, Anu Koivunen, Shuruq Naguib and Sandhya Shukla, all of whom have discussed the book with me, either when it was still germinating in my mind, or in its later stages. Several others have commented on drafts of chapters included in this book. Many thanks to Suki Ali, Mark Johnson, Maureen McNeil, Nayanika Mookherjee, Sarah Neal, Lynne Pearce, Geraldine Pratt, Andrew Sayer, Divya Tolia-Kelly, Jackie Stacey, as well as two anonymous reviewers. I am particularly grateful to Anne Cronin, Gail Lewis, and Kate Nash, each of whom has patiently read several chapters in various stages of completion. The support of all these people and their belief in my project has been immeasurable. And to Cynthia Weber, for the numerous conversations about this project, and for her reading of several versions of the manuscript and her invariably frank and astute advice. Cindy also lovingly and patiently witnessed the fluctuations of my own 'feeling states' as I worked through this project – and, always the caring person, would know how and when to calm me or make me laugh, most often both.

I am also indebted to my students from my undergraduate course, *Nation, Migration, Multiculturalism*, whose inquisitiveness and occasional scepticism have challenged me in the most productive and engaging ways, and to my PhD students, past and present, who remain a constant source of inspiration. Elements of this book were presented and tried out in several conferences and seminars in the UK and elsewhere – too numerous to list here. I wish to thank all those who patiently listened for their interest and for their engaged questions. Each occasion proved to be enabling and encouraging, and allowed me to sharpen and refine my thoughts.

This book was completed thanks to a sabbatical leave provided by the Sociology Department at Lancaster University. I had the great fortune to spend that time at the University of Arizona, Tucson, where I was housed in the Institute for Lesbian, Gay, Bisexual and Transgender Studies. Special thanks to Eithne Luibhéid for her warm and enthusiastic welcome, and for the many lovely times we had together. And I thank Eithne and Caren Zimmerman for ensuring that my sojourn ran as smoothly as could be. And thanks, Caren, for your interest in the 'faces of Britain'. One of the highlights of my stay in Tucson was the meetings with the 'Subjectivies, Sexualities and Political Cultures' research cluster, which always provided welcome intellectual relief and a break away from my computer; thanks to Laura Briggs, Liz Kennedy, Adam Geary, Laura Gutiérrez, Miranda Joseph, Sandra Soto, Eithne Luibhéid, Spike Peterson, and Hai Ren for those stimulating, challenging, generous, and always fun conversations. I am proud to be part of (and to have been present at the inception of) what we shall now fondly call 'the Tucson School'. It's a treat when friendships develop out of academic exchanges, and I can only hope that I will not have to wait too long to see our *clusterista* friends again. Finally, many thanks to the Chorover family, in Tucson, whose house we rented: I couldn't have wished for a more inspiring and delightful setting. I am now totally seduced by the southern Arizona desert!

Thanks to John Urry, series editor, and Gerhard Boomgaarden, senior editor at Routledge, for their swift and excited response to my initial book proposal, which gave me the confidence to engage in this long endeavour. Ann Carter and Jason Mitchell, respectively editorial assistant and production editor at Routledge, have been very helpful in assisting me with the final editing of the manuscript. I also greatly appreciated Janet MacMillan's thorough and professional copy editing of the manuscript. I take full responsibility for any remaining odd phrasing or Gallicism in the text – which I most likely chose to keep there.

As ever, I thank my family in Canada, Monique Fortier, Claude Fortier and Marie Labelle, for supporting me in ways that reach deeper than they can imagine. This book is dedicated to my late father Robert Fortier, who taught me so much about respect and integrity, about outrage at social injustices, and about understanding and questioning how privilege works; and who taught me how to appreciate and remain amazed by *les petits plaisirs de la vie* – life's simple pleasures – that make up the fabric of everyday life.

And finally, Cindy, with whom the everyday is a big pleasure of life.

Some of the chapters were published previously in different versions and are reprinted here with permission from the publishers. An earlier version of Chapter 2 appeared as 'Pride politics and multiculturalist citizenship', in *Ethnic and Racial Studies* 28(3), 2005. A skeletal version of Chapter 4 was published with the title 'Too close for comfort: loving thy neighbour and the management of multicultural intimacies', *Environment and Planning D: Society and Space* 25, 2007, pp. 104–19, (London: Pion Limited).

1   Horizons of intimacies

[T]he multicultural is a constitutive form of Western national entanglement which has profound deconstructive implications for how we understand the politics of national identity. It produces the paradox of the multicultural impossibility of full national representation.

(Hesse 1999: 206)

The objection I have to multiculturalism is that multiculturalism is in effect saying that it is impossible to have an Australian ethos, that it is impossible to have a common Australian culture.

(Australian Prime Minister John Howard in 1989, cited in Beams 2004)

So it is not that we need to dispense with multicultural Britain. On the contrary we should continue celebrating it.

(British Prime Minister Tony Blair 2006)

How can we conceive of 'multiculture' in ways that address the complexities and intensities of feelings that it invariably ignites? Since its emergence as state-sponsored policy in the fourth report of the Canadian Royal Commission on Bilingualism and Biculturalism in 1969 (CRCBB 1969),[1] 'multiculturalism' has had a chequered 'diasporic career' (Bennett 1998: 2), appearing at the heart of national debates about the future of national cultures and identities in a globalizing world. From its early Canadian incarnation as a integrationist (read anti-assimilationist) 'mosaic' strategy in 1970 – which was also a nationalist strategy of distinguishing Canadian policy from the US melting-pot policy – multiculturalism has taken on numerous inflections, celebratory or condemnatory, and has been at the heart of debates about the preservation of equality, social cohesion, and national unity. Today, the discourse about multiculturalism is in turmoil in several Western countries and it appears that its days as a state-sponsored strategy are numbered.[2] To be sure, multiculturalism has manifold meanings that are situated in various historical, political, and socio-cultural contexts. Struggles over exclusion, discrimination, and recognition of people minoritized on the basis of race, ethnicity, and to a lesser extent, gender, sexuality, class, or disability have variously been mobilized in the name of multiculturalism. Its deployment in government strategies and social policies also vary from context to context and is always subject to intense debates over the preferred mode of incorporating (ethnic) minorities, such as integrationist, assimilationist, or hyphenated (c.f. Alexander 2001). For critical multiculturalists – who have pointedly emphasized the power dynamics constitutive of, and reproduced by, multiculturalisms – multiculturalism is a floating signifier (Goldberg 1994; Gunew 2004; Hesse 1999, 2000); the term 'has no essence' as Shohat and Stam put it (1994: 47). In short, and as Barnor Hesse puts it, multiculturalism is a highly 'contested frame of reference for thinking about the quotidian of cohesion of western civil societies uncertain about their national and ethnic futures' (2000: 1). In all their different guises and throughout their agitated histories, multiculturalist politics of the national future have come to define the urgencies of the present.

This is perhaps nowhere more apparent than in contemporary Britain. The sheer volume of debates, consultations, analyses, editorials, and images circulating around multiculturalism in the British public sphere since the turn of the millennium makes it impossible not to notice how unsettled and unsettling 'multicultural Britain' is. From a national outpouring of pride in Britain's multicultural character in October 2000, to policy guidelines for more intercultural mixing within neighbourhoods as the antidote against racial violence in 2001, to the chairman of the Commission for Racial Equality, Trevor Phillips, declaring in 2004 that the term should be discarded because it fosters separatism, to debates over wearing the jilbab in schools in 2005, to the shock and horror that came with the realization that the perpetrators of the attacks on London's transport system in 2005 were 'children of multicultural Britain', through to the then Leader of the House of Commons Jack Straw's 'discomfort' about Muslim women wearing the face veil, the niqab, in 2006 – all of which decidedly brought multiculturalism and 'integration' to the forefront of passionate public and political debate. My purpose is to try to understand what it was that these and other events in contemporary Britain triggered in the national imaginary, and how 'the multicultural' was deployed in these moments. Taking seriously the question about how we could conceive of multiculture in ways that address the intensities of feelings it ignites, this volume examines the ways in which contemporary Britain is (re)imagined as a multicultural nation and how these imaginings are invested with idea(l)s of mixing, loving thy neighbour, and feelings for the nation.

The chapters that follow track the multiple incarnations and transformations 'multiculture' has undergone between 2000 and 2006 and they are premised on an understanding of 'multiculture' as a key site where the politics and culture of the nation are embattled. The central argument underpinning this book is that rather than accepting 'multicultural Britain' as an inescapable fact, it is to be conceived as a *horizon* – a vision, an imaginary that is grounded in variously localized conceptions of the 'real' world (more on horizons below). In political and in some theoretical discourses, multiculturalism remains widely conceived as a response to cultural and demographic diversification in particular geographical contexts, whether the term is used in a descriptive manner – equated with the 'fact' of diversity – or in a reflexive manner – as a deliberate managerial approach to diversity. However, insofar as multiculturalism is an intensely 'contested frame of reference' and a 'broad political imaginary' (Hesse 2000: 1, 9), multiculturalism is not so much a policy and governing *response* to the 'realities' of cultural and ethno-racial pluralism, as it is an *ideal* aimed at the achievement of well-managed diversity (c.f. Mitchell 2004). Hence, multiculturalism *constructs* visions of 'the multicultural' as much as it is informed by historically specific visions that circulate in the wider public sphere. I consider 'multiculture' as something which is put to work, which is mobilized to produce desires, identities, anxieties, and so on, in the reconfiguration of what connects inhabitants of the national space to one another, as well as to the nation itself.[3] A vivid example is the way that 'the multicultural' was celebrated on 6 July 2005 as one of the main reasons why London succeeded in its bid for the 2012 Olympics. On the following tragic day,[4] 'multicultural Britain' became a weapon against terrorism and against those sections of the population who hate, as Tony Blair recently put it, 'everything the Olympic bid symbolized', that is, 'a compelling, modern vision of Britain: a country at ease with different races, religions and cultures' (Blair 2006). Debates around the benefits and failures of multiculturalism were reanimated by 7/7, and the weeks that followed saw several critiques, namely from Conservative quarters, blaming it for fostering national disunity and for being the root cause of the attacks in London because of its benevolence and soft-touch approach to cultural difference.

These intense debates are indicative of the extent to which multiculturalism fosters dreams or anxieties about the nation's present and future. In this regard, the phrase 'multicultural horizons' refers to the intricate process of simultaneous *witnessing*, *questioning*, and *imagining*: witnessing that the 'we' *are* multicultural (and always have been; see Chapter 2), questioning how to achieve 'integration with diversity' (Home Office 2001c; Blair 2006), and imagining the future of the multicultural nation. These deliberations may cast the nation/al in different temporalities – the past, present, and future – but they all meet in their quest to understand who the national 'we' is, what it means at this particular moment in time, and what the limits of the nation/al are. For this reason, they should be read as simultaneous moments that extend into each other in the emergence of a spatial-temporal horizon where the politics and culture of the nation are embattled in the name of multicultural presents and futures. I elaborate on the concept of horizons in the second section of this chapter. But first, I situate questions raised in this book within the wider historical conjuncture that necessitates a version of multiculturalism that is primarily concerned with the management of what I call 'multicultural intimacies'.

Multicultural intimacies

Multicultural Horizons offers an account of how mutating definitions of Britishness are intertwined with changing understandings of living with difference. Readers of this volume will find that different versions of multiculturalism coexist and at times intermesh in the contemporary British public domain; versions that assume or require different types of intercultural contact that would achieve 'multicultural Britain' – assimilationist, differentialist, integrationist, sexual, platonic, friendly and neighbourly, indifferent, antagonistic, cognitive, educational, mutual. Multiculturalism entails shifting the mechanics of creating national communities by presenting new national family portraits that suggest a substantive shift in who 'we' are and how 'we' relate to each other. This shift is part of a wider search for new grammars for national identity that prescribe forms of being together informed by particular visions of the multicultural nation. The central question pervading this exploration is threefold: what kinds of connections and identifications are required of and between inhabitants in a multicultural nation, on what grounds, and what are the limits?

This question seeks to capture some of the deep anxieties and issues that have arisen in recent years and that have been addressed under the banner of 'multiculturalism'. Since the late twentieth century, an anti-multiculturalist backlash has been gaining ground in several Western countries, leading a number of governments to retreat from state-sponsored multiculturalism (see note 2). The general point of critique is against policies and programmes that aim at integrating minorities and immigrant populations and which are said to be differentialist and separatist rather than unifying. This critique reduces multiculturalism to being nothing but an endorsement of what is widely conceived as the separatist 'politics of difference' of the last 30 years. What interests me here is not whether this constitutes a drift away from the 'spirit of multiculturalism' (Mitchell 2006: 392) aimed at providing individuals with a strong sense of self-worth, towards a more privatized multiculturalism founded on individual duty, skills, mobility and self-management. Rather, I am interested in the kinds of anxieties that this critique itself is indicative of in the context of the war on terror, on the one hand, and of what Aiwha Ong calls the 'desacralization of state membership' (Ong 2006: 145), on the other.

The war on terror has brought security to the fore of the neo-liberal agenda, with fears being exacerbated, after the attacks in London in July 2005, by the realization that 'the enemy' can come as much from within as from without the national borders – a point that I discuss more fully in Chapter 3. The point that I wish to emphasize at this stage is that the global war on terror is cast within what Mahmood Mamdani calls the 'culturalization' of political conflict (in Brown 2006: 167), epitomized in Samuel Huntington's theory of the 'clash of civilizations' (Huntington 1996). The assumption is that cultural difference rather than ideology is a site of natural hostility and separation in a post-Cold-War era. The contemporary liberal project is to resolve that problem by ensuring that culture is kept separate from politics and from the autonomous subject-citizen. The idea is that the citizen is 'prior to culture and free to choose culture' and that 'politics is above culture and free of culture' (Brown 2006: 167). Culture is something to be enjoyed, consumed at will and with discernment by the autonomous liberal subject. 'Culture', in short, is a bias – not necessarily a negative bias, but still, a bias that distorts the running of a good civil society, and as such, is potentially dangerous. In the context of the international war on terror, the culturalization of political conflict works to distinguish between the 'modern' liberals who 'make culture and are its masters', and the pre-modern non-liberal societies that are merely conduits of their culture (Mamdani in Brown 2006: 20). Similarly, a culturalist argument about ethnic conflict underpins contemporary multiculturalist politics that seek to manage and negotiate cultural, ethnic, and religious differences and to avoid them erupting into public life. In this context, when 'culture' and 'migrant' or 'ethnic minority' meet, 'culture' is conceived in primordialist terms – naturalized, privatized, and ruling over 'deep feelings'. When 'culture' and 'citizenship' meet, 'culture' is diluted and swept under the banner of more laudable and 'universal' values. But it is not simply a matter of saying that 'they' have cultures, 'we' have values, as I suggest elsewhere (2006; also Sandercock 2003). As Wendy Brown pointedly argues, the distinction is drawn between 'us' *having* culture and enjoying it, and 'them' *being* culture and being ruled by it (2006: 151). 'We' *have* culture, 'they' *are* culture; 'we' are citizens, 'they' are a people.

Many neo-liberal Western states, including Britain, adopt a rhetoric of the national bond that emphasizes the 'glue of values' rather than the 'glue of ethnicity' (Goodhart 2004). In other words, contemporary Western states have taken a turn toward tolerance, integration, and diversity in which mechanisms of regulation, administration, control, and disciplining of the population work to conjure up classificatory schemes of inclusion and exclusion on the basis of values rather than on displays of cultural competence and capital. One of the effects of the language of values is to conceal the historical articulations that constitute them as universal, timeless, and unquestionable. This politics of values inflects 'cultural racism' with a moral undertone: a kind of *moral racism* in which the terms of racism have shifted into a new arrangement – emphasis on values and their impact on degrees of differences attributed to different groups – while the focus remains the same – ethnic minorities and the maintenance of white hegemony, the form of which is changing in relation to the particular historical conditions that impact on its definition, such as the international war on terror, the rise of state concerns for national security, and the European-wide questioning of assimilation and integration. Thus, for example, the taxonomic shift in Britain, from 'ethnic minorities' in the 1970s to 'minority faith communities' today, is fundamentally entangled with the new moral politics that produce a new inflection of cultural racism in which beliefs, values, and morals are the primary site for the marking of absolute difference, rather than 'cultural practices' such as customs, traditions, and 'lifestyles'. The difference between 'traditions' and 'values' is thin and slippery, and the distinction I offer between 'cultural racism' and 'moral racism' is analytical rather than intended to reflect a clear-cut separation. But it points to the ways in which religion specifically figures as a marker of difference, and where some groups are seen as more saturated by their religious beliefs than others – the liberal, a-cultural citizen is one who practices religion, but is not ruled by it. Concealed in the sanctification of values as universal is their historical construction through ethnicized and racialized conceptions of what constitutes appropriate, 'civilized' behaviour. Values grow out of historically-specific settings, and the worthiness of values is assessed in terms of behaviours which are seen as *expressions* of whole cultures and lifestyles which, in turn, are conceived as ruling the lives of 'ethnic' minorities. Values work as technologies of regulation – the regulation of aversion, in Wendy Brown's words (2006) – that may conditionally and provisionally allow what is unwanted or deviant. Within this moral politics, the problem of living together becomes a problem of 'them' not only adjusting to 'our' values, but, as Blair stated in December 2006, of 'them' making it their *duty* to embrace the nation's values such as tolerance, because that is what 'makes Britain, Britain' (Blair 2006).

The 'desacralization of state membership' (Ong 2006: 145), for its part, results from the perceived destructive effects on the sacred national bond, of diversity caused by transnationalisms and internationalizations, which is what multiculture is widely associated with (more on this in the next section). In an article that caused much controversy in 2004, the editor of *Prospect* magazine, David Goodhart, stated that tolerance is a symptom that 'we [the UK] don't care enough about each other to resent the arrival of the other' (2004: 25). Likewise in 2005, Leo Benedictus suggested in the *Guardian* that 'Londoners resent immigrants less than they might ... because they have so few values left to be threatened' (2005: 2). Thus Goodhart and Benedictus turn tolerance into a sign of the nation's weakness and an affront to the nation's narcissistic love: we should resent the other and the diversity he/she brings for he/she pulls us away from ourselves. Goodhart is mourning the loss of ourselves as the objects of mutual care and love. By extension, he is mourning the loss of the nation – as a community of people who look, act, and behave alike – as *the* object/site of attachment.

In this context, the revived critiques against the separatist tendencies of multiculturalism are not so much stressing concerns about cultural provincialism and relativism at the expense of national cultural unity – which sum up several anti-multiculturalists complaints of the 1980s (see Eller 1997) – as they are concerned with *adherence* and *allegiance* to a single nation(-state), and with reclaiming the values of patriotism as the way to secure national cohesion. Put simply, the issue of multicultural integration is not so much about the respect of *cultural identity* and the protection of self-worth, as it is about *identification* with and within a single and unitary nation. This is a politics that 'turns the nation into a privatized state of feeling' (Berlant 1997: 11). As I argue in Chapter 5, a great deal of political attention, concern, and effort goes into the 'internal states' of some citizens – how do you feel, *at heart*?

These concerns dovetail into a popular trope in futuristic visions of internal diversification: the trope of crowdedness and intensified closeness (consider how the numbers debate is always a feature of arguments about immigration). A few months before he became Prime Minister, when he was Chancellor of the Exchequer, Gordon Brown stated: 'the 21st-century world will be characterised by peoples of different nationalities living *closer to each other* and having to find ways to live together' (G. Brown 2007; emphasis added). Multiculturalism has become more than a strategy aimed at achieving managed diversity – be it in material or symbolic terms, in terms of human rights, equality, social justice, or the politics of recognition, or in terms of integration, assimilation, or hyphenation. Multiculturalism is also about the conception of non-physical relationships in terms of a spatial social imaginary that requires the management of physical, cultural, emotive (namely identificatory) proximities between inhabitants: it is about multicultural intimacies.

In other words, multicultural politics are invested in cultivating feelings within and for the nation, often at the expense of examining the legacies and inequalities of racialized, gendered, sexualized, class histories. What kinds of affects, then, are cultivated in the name of multiculture? The materials discussed in the next chapters are scrutinized for the ways in which they discursively *emplace* individuals within webs of social or institutional multicultural interactions that prescribe ways of living together and feeling for each other. Multicultural encounters are not only negotiated and 'managed' in literal spatial form ('linking projects' bussing school children between 'ethnic' or 'faith' schools, various government 'capacity building' strategies to regenerate multi-ethnic neighbourhoods, etc.), but *these relations are imagined through specific emotional and ethical injunctions*, such as mixing, tolerance, 'embracing the other' (Blunkett 2001), and loving thy neighbour. Moreover, these injunctions are imagined in the ambivalent spatial terms of *obligations to* and *dangers of* proximity. 'Intimacy' thus extends beyond kinship or friendship to other forms of closeness – geo-graphical, cultural, communitarian – that are given substance in terms of obligations to, and dangers of, proximity. Multiculturalism is decidedly about proximity,[5] intimacy, and feelings *for* and *within* the nation.

Multicultural Horizons draws out the register of intimacy – the register of physical, cognitive, and emotional closeness – deployed in political dis-courses and public debates and representations of multiculture. Multi-culturalism is not only predicated on suppressing or managing immigrants' and ethnic minorities' feelings (such as their attachment to their home-land), but the language of multiculture is always filtered through an ethos of intimacy and closeness that prescribes for *everyone* (not only minorities and immigrants) the criteria for responsible 'caring' citizenship[6] which establish the limits of a 'civil' nation. In Britain and in Europe, strategies for fostering social cohesion are one example where states seeks to engi-neer modes of living together that draw on languages of intimacy, close-ness, and feelings for the nation as a panacea to social conflict. As a British Home Office document put it, 'We need to ensure that *all* citizens feel a sense of pride in being British and a sense of belonging to this country *and to each other*' (Home Office 2004a: 6; emphasis added). This book con-cerns itself with how such discourses of intimate multiculturalism 'exude fabricated sociality' (Herzfeld 1997: 7) and 'animate and enflesh [national] love, sociality and bodies' (Povinelli 2006: 3). That is, the texts I engage address readers as agents who are variously and inter-subjectively inter-pellated, positioned, and materialized through the very publicness of feel-ings for the nation and the *idea* that there is a community, or several communities, of feeling to be encouraged, sustained, achieved, or dis-mantled and excised.[7] What kinds of intimacy are deployed and in what terms? What models of closeness circulate, and at what time does a new model become imperative? What counts as legitimate intimacy? What kinds of intimacies or connections between inhabitants in a multicultural nation are promoted, on what grounds, and how do they relate to (new) forms of othering? In Ann Laura Stoler's (2001) evocative phrase, *Multi-cultural Horizons* attends to those 'tense and tender ties' that are knotted into the national fantasy of multicultural Britain.

The analysis draws attention to experiences, feelings, and opinions that dominant public discourses simultaneously produce and occlude for those who are positioned variously as models, threats or (un/willing) hosts within multicultural Britain. This is where national cohesion might be conceived in terms that are not necessarily modelled on, say, friendship (Derrida 1997) or comradeship (Anderson 1991: 6), but that could take the form of genial indifference (Tonkiss 2003; Chapter 4 in this volume). This is also where I show how intimacy is not reducible to closeness; it can also be the site of distancing, alienation, anxiety, dis/identification, dis/ease, violence, and hate.

Paramount here are the imperial and colonial legacies that provide the discursive limits of *both* multiculturalism and intimacy. The deconstructive impulse of multiculturalism that Barnor Hesse insists upon in the first epi-graph, tackles head on:

> [the] racialised logic of modernity that projects through its Western circulation an ontological distinction between 'Europe–whiteness–masculinity' and 'Non-Europe–non-whiteness–femininity' … where the former reflects singular normativity and the latter comparative pathology. It is this process of racialisation that inaugurates the dis-crepant formation of multiculturalism.
>
> (Hesse 1999: 207)

Discrepant multiculturalism excavates the repressed and disavowed 'points of entanglement' that multiculturalism signifies – such as the dis-avowal of enduring imperial implications in articulations of difference that continue to shore up the hegemonic construction of whiteness/European-ness as the universal (c.f. McClintock 1995; Seshadri-Crooks 2000). But the meanings of 'Europeanness' and of 'whiteness' are not as uniform as Hesses's theory suggests. They are unstable and they change over time and across different contexts. For example, indigeneity in Australia and Canada is mediated by a history of British colonialism that has con-temporary implications in articulations of multiculturalism, and in claims of Europeanness (Gunew 2004). In Britain, in contrast, multiculturalism arose within the political and intellectual ferment surrounding the migra-tion of colonial subjects 'back home', to England – questioning the roots of Englishness and forcing a reassessment of what it means to be English or British. In contemporary Britain, the empire occupies an ambivalent place within Britain's relationship not only with post-war migrants who constitute today's 'settled' communities, but also with new migrants hailing from outside the British Empire. For Paul Gilroy (2004a), the pre-sent political climate in Britain is best understood as a post-colonial mel-ancholia where the nation is struggling with the distress caused by the realization of the Empire's violence and abuses, while there is also a desire to remember the Empire as a source of national pride and accomplishment. In Chapter 2, I consider how the ambivalence and struggle inherent in melancholia is at play in attempts to write a guilt-free version of the national story. More broadly, Britain's melancholic state constitutes the context surrounding the particular historical conjuncture that allows for specific versions of multicultural horizon to arise in the UK now.[8] Insofar as narcissism is a constitutive feature of melancholia, the ambivalent rela-tionship to the love-object (the Empire) is also about the ambivalent rela-tionship to the national self.[9] This volume attends to various ways in which the contested meanings of multiculture that circulate in the public domain have, to various degrees, the preservation of national self-love at heart. What strategies of dis/avowal are deployed to ensure the endurance of national love?

A further 'crisis' identified under the banner of multiculturalism is the consequence of the unexpected effects of *post-colonial intimacy*, where the constitutive outside is now inside and 'integrated' (Blair 2006); she/he has 'developed' like us (Chapter 3). In this context, other disavowals of empire are at work in the articulations of modes of intimacy which are also deeply anchored in European imperialism (Povinelli 2006; Stoler 1995, 2002). I am agnostic about the extent to which the modern Western nation is primarily anchored in technologies of race (Hesse 1999; Bhabha 1994) or in technologies of sex (Foucault 1979, 1997), or whether both racial and sexual classifications '*shared* their emergence with the bourgeois order of the early nineteenth century' (Stoler 2002: 143–44). But what I take from this scholarship is that multicultural intimacies are points of entanglement that are not only inscribed in a series of inclusions and exclusions – where excess is merely that which is left out – but they are also etched in the *desire* for the other while keeping him/her at a 'proper distance' (Sharma 2006: 106). *Multicultural Horizons* excavates this double process of *rapprochement* and distancing, of embracing and repelling, as it operates differently on different bodies – for not all minoritized subjects are othered in the same terms. Who is close to whom, to what extent, and what are the limits? This question diverts the attention slightly beside race and ethnicity, which remain the privileged signifiers of difference in multiculturalism discourse, towards additional issues of gender, sex, and generations. The latter takes us to questions of kinship which 'become sites of intense displacement for other political fears ... about new demographics, and about the very unity and transmissibility of the nation' (Butler 2002: 21). Indeed, the heterosexuality and 'generationality' of multiculture stand widely uninterrogated in the vast literature on multiculturalism. *Multicultural Horizons* aims to fill this gap by examining the ways in which anxieties about the multicultural present get figured through kinship and familial practices that become some of the modalities through which race, ethnicity, as well as class, are hierarchized.[10]

Horizons, fantasy, and structures of feeling

The following chapters offer insights into the prevailing national structure of feeling (Williams 1977; Edensor 2002) and the social anxieties that dominate much of the British public domain in the early years of the twenty-first century. My archive is made up of a range of different types of documents – policy and consultation documents emanating for the most part from the Home Office, reports and debates in the national press, photographic stills, and documentary. This 'transindividual and multi-institutional archive of images and statements' (Shohat and Stam 1994: 18) produces various ways of imagining and understanding 'multicultural Britain'. Together, these materials are indicative of the contemporary 'cultural moment' while they also constitute a polysemic and shifting cultural formation; the discourses and meanings they produce are by no means homogeneous, nor is my analysis in any way comprehensive of all the themes and issues that come under the banner of 'multicultural Britain'. Nor am I suggesting that the sum of the texts I engage equals the meaning of being British today. But they all go into the making of what Derek Gregory refers to as 'public cultures of assumption, disposition and action' (Gregory 2004: 28). Put simply, the analysis attends to the *sense* of the nation as it is conveyed in the public domain at a particular historical conjuncture, and concerns itself with two interwoven processes: the structur*ing* of feeling, and the formation and sustenance of a national fantasy.

First, in the spirit of Raymond Williams's legacy, the following analysis attends to the ways in which feelings for, and within, the nation are mediated and structured in various forms of representation and enunciative strategies.[11] I do so by scrutinizing how the indeterminacy of multicultural Britain is negotiated and resolved within various normative formulations that prescribe ways of 'being together' within the national frame. More specifically, I focus on how the unsettling effects of multiculture are stabilized: on the one hand through racial, gendered, sexualized, class, and generational systems of differentiation and categorization, and on the other, through prescriptions of what constitutes 'proper' forms of interaction between, across, as well as within these differences as they are deployed in the register of intimacy, closeness, and community of feeling. In this way I am gesturing towards the ways in which *all* British 'nationals' are summoned into good citizenship founded on criteria of civility that are variously conjured up or formalized in various sites of the public domain. Pride, moderation, loving thy neighbour, mixing, all are cast within normative discourses around which the limits of the civil nation are drawn. How they then impact on local or institutional practices and individuals' perceptions, dispositions, and actions is not my concern.[12] My point is that we must pay attention to the work that these discourses do, the premises they are founded upon, and the issues at stake in the call for particular kinds of relations.

The second strand of the argument that buttresses this study is an acknowledgment of the structures of feeling as investing in, and invested by, a national fantasy; that is, the material gathered in this volume is constitutive of a cultural formation through which the fantasy structure of the nation is sustained and (re)formulated. Lauren Berlant (1991, 1997) has famously shown how the nation is a fantasy that is brought into being in the public domain by repeatedly imagining that it exists and iterating it as something real, out there, that binds the 'national people' together. Fantasy, here, is more than its popular conception suggests – as escape, make-believe, whimsical fabrication. Rather, it is a 'protective fiction', as Freud put it (in Rose 1996: 5), a narrative support, a story that gives consistency to the nation and its subjects. The national fantasy is embattled through connections to 'the real', which is said to be in need of improvement or correction (Hage 1997; Hesse 1999). In Lacanian terms, a fantasy structure supports the minimum idealization necessary for the subject to constitute a *sense* of reality; the frame through which reality can be assessed (Salecl 2004: 24). In this sense, fantasy is not an escape from social reality, but rather its necessary 'psychic glue' (Rose 1996: 3) which protects the nation/al from the horrors of the 'real' that threaten the disintegration of the self; it keeps it whole.[13] The second and third epigraphs opening this chapter are a case in point. Both are manifestations of political 'imaginaries [that] articulate a conception of the nation through the multicultural' (Hesse 1999: 216). In the first epigraph, Hesse points to the deconstructive force of the multicultural as it threatens to unravel the fantasy of the national whole because in the multicultural, the supplementary minority insinuates itself within the nation and the national subject and antagonizes its assumed power of generalization and full representation. This is precisely what John Howard is concerned about, though in contrast to Hesse, the former Australian Prime Minister believes in the national whole as a thing that is bound through the 'common Australian culture'. Tony Blair, for his part, also believes in the national, but one where the multicultural is constitutive rather than disruptive excess: the fantasy of a *multicultural* Britain. This is a national self that is imagined as *multi* – be it multinational (G. Brown 2007) or multi-cultural (Blair 2006). Not *e pluribus unum*, but rather 'integration *with* diversity' (c.f. Home Office 2001c; Blair 2006; emphasis added). The concept of multicultural intimacies addresses the blurring of boundaries and the constant movement of feelings between Self and Other that interrupts nation/al certainty. At the same time, 'multicultural intimacy' is conceived here as a narrative strategy to sustain the fantasy of national wholeness; a fantasy that protects the nation against the destructive effects of splitting the national self.[14] Thus, a specific question arises from Blair's multicultural horizon: what happens to the fantasy of national culture when multiculture and those imagined as constituting the 'multicultural' are not only 'let in', but conceived as *integral* to the nation and the national 'body' itself (c.f. Ahmed 2000)? What is the 'psychic glue' of *this* version of national fantasy made of, and what are its limits? And what happens when the 'psychic glue' unravels, for instance in the face of the uncannily familiar who turns out to be an 'enemy within' (Chapter 3)?

Both Blair and Howard are evoking a nation constituted by the desire for a national community and identity, rather than surfacing from an already constituted identity. This is what an analysis of multicultural horizons as a political fantasy aims to get at: the desires, anxieties, fears, and dreams that invest the national structure of feeling. I choose the term 'horizon' over 'imagination'[15] because the former includes the latter but is not reducible to it. 'Horizons' connote dreams and visions (as in Blair's 'vision' of 'New Britain') while they also conjure up images that include some imagined 'ground' or terrain 'where place meets sky', as the MS

Word Encarta Dictionary informs me. It also teaches me that in geography, horizon refers to a distinct layer of soil, the characteristics of which distinguish it from other layers. The three 'layers' constitutive of multicultural horizons – witnessing, questioning, imagining – draw attention to the varying relations between the national imaginary/dreamscape, on the one hand, and perceived localized practices 'on the ground' on the other, and to how these varying relations solidify into something that becomes real. In other words, if states appropriate idioms of intimacy and closeness for their own purposes of commanding loyalty and allegiance (Berlant 1997, 2000), they also draw on imagined localized practices – be they figured in communities, neighbourhoods, or individuals – as models of national character or as sources of national embarrassment (Herzfeld 1997).[16] Thus, as Judith Butler puts it, state 'regulations do not always seek to order what exists but to figure social life in certain imaginary ways. The incommensurability between state stipulation and existing social life means that this gap must be covered over for the state to continue to exercise its authority and to exemplify the kind of coherence that it is expected to confer on its subjects' (2002: 28; also Rose 1996). These discursive moves are constitutive of the fantasy structure of the nation/al as a community of feeling.

The spatial connotations of 'horizons' can be further brought to bear in thinking about how the imaginative geographies of multiculturalism not only emerge in that tension between localized practices and national imaginaries, but they are also outer-national. As a 'global discourse' (Gunew 2004: 15), multiculturalism has its own transnational circulation. First, from Nathan Glazer's declaration that 'We are all Multiculturalists Now' (1997), to the Benetton effect of corporate multiculturalism adopted by transnational companies who 'pretend to be the new regionally global guardians of multicultural justice' (Matuštík 1998: 114; also Žižek 1997), multiculturalism developed in the 1990s as part and parcel of a neo-liberal political economy that commodifies diversity as a valuable asset (economic, political, and social) that deserves proper management and attention. Second, the transnationalism of multiculturalism is also manifest in its increased circulation in contexts beyond those countries traditionally associated with multiculture (Canada, Australia, and the US). Several European countries are now debating multiculturalism (Grillo and Pratt 2002; Longley and Kiberd 2001; Saharso 2003; Tuori 2007), while multiculturalism has been integral to European Union (EU) politics and strategies of integration of EU and non-EU migrants (Mitchell 2006; Modood and Werbner 1997; Modood *et al.* 2005). Third, multiculturalism is a discourse *about* globalization insofar as it is (somewhat reductively) conceived as resulting from immigration, diasporic affiliations, transnational corporate connections, the internationalization of higher education, or international trade agreements that allow for the 'free' movement of skilled labourers. Thus the fact that 'the multicultural' is *necessarily* transnational – that it is always cast as the effect of 'global' and external forces – accentuates its national trait. These expanding (the global) and contracting (the national) poles of the multicultural should not distract us from the fact multicultural horizons are ultimately inward looking. Multiculturalism is an introspective process aimed at strengthening a nation (or a conglomerate of nations, such as the EU) in its struggles against perceived world forces that produce internal diversification.

Encarta adds that in the plural form, 'horizons' refer to the range or limits of somebody's interests, knowledge, or experience. This definition, however, confines horizons to the past tense given the connotations of 'experience' and 'knowledge'. Rather, thinking of horizons as a structure of feeling points to a 'practical consciousness of a present kind ... a social experience which is still *in process* ... but which in analysis ... has its emergent, connecting, and dominant characteristics, indeed its specific *hierarchies*' (Williams 1977: 132; second emphasis added). Often not recognized as historical but rather taken to be unique to 'the national', multicultural horizons are organized around specific structures of feeling, specific hierarchies of feeling, that are presented as testimonies to the true values of Britishness.

Finally, 'horizons' are about infinity; about the infinite possibilities offered by a dreamlike or nightmare fantasy. Nightmare fantasies of crime, disease, or national annihilation as a result of countries being 'swamped' by excessive and unmanageable numbers of (unwanted) immigrants intermesh with dreamlike fantasies of the powers of the national bond as the path towards the harmonious integration of the nation's varied communities. Integration and immigration control meet in multicultural horizons, though the ways in which they articulate varies significantly between countries. Still, the alignment of integration and immigration are widely framed within a 'host–stranger' relation that set the limits of the 'civil' nation. The questions that these dreamlike or nightmare fantasies raise concern the limits of tolerance – be it in terms of acceptance, or in terms of infrastructural and institutional capacity – and the preservation of decency – the right to 'decent' living conditions or the protection of 'decent' citizens. In other words, multicultural horizons are not only about shaping and protecting national identity, but are also about forging particular conceptions of civility. As this book documents, at stake in imaginings of multicultural Britain is the preservation of a particular version of British civility as it is deployed through various prescribed forms of sociality.[17]

Diversity and the limits of multicultural Britain

In June 2006, Ruth Kelly, who was then Communities Secretary, launched the Commission for Integration and Cohesion.[18] In her speech, she expressed her sympathy for:

[those] white Britons who do not feel comfortable with change. They see the shops and restaurants changing. They see their town and neighbourhoods becoming more diverse. Detached from the benefits of those changes, they begin to believe stories about ethnic minorities getting special treatment, and to develop a resentment, a sense of grievance ... We have moved from a period of uniform consensus on the value of multiculturalism to one where we can encourage a debate by questioning whether it is encouraging separateness ... In our attempt to avoid imposing a single British identity and culture, have we ended up with some communities living in isolation of each other?

(Kelly 2006)

Kelly's words sum up several issues taken up in this book. First, they aptly illustrate the ways in which the local arena is used to procure a particular understanding of wider, national issues. The texts I engage in the following chapters depict various personal or communal forms of intimacy – from personal feelings for the nation, to individual/ized forms of inter-cultural mixing – that onlookers are called upon to witness as manifestations of the state of the changing nation.

Second, her concern about the discomfort of white Britons shifts the attention to the comfort of the *white* nation/al and away from that of the minoritized subjects that some versions multiculturalism have aimed at (for example, as one of the founding principles of 'multicultural education'). In establishing an explicit distinction between the uncomfortable white Britons and the upsetting non-whites, Kelly is decidedly situating the origins of diversity and of discomfort on the non-white body. I use non-white deliberately here, to emphasize how 'Whiteness' is 'the Universal', the master signifier of accomplished citizenship. As Kalpana Seshadri-Crooks (2000) argues, 'Whiteness' (capital 'W') is more than about skin colour. 'Whiteness' is about race as a regime of looking; a regime of observing, classifying, and judging based on norms of behaviour that are inflected by class, sexuality, gender, age. 'Whiteness' is the master signifier in 'a signifying chain that ... provides subjects with certain symbolic positions such as "black", "white", "Asian", etc., in *relation* to the master signifier' (Seshadri-Crooks 2000: 4; emphasis added). This book attends to the limits of 'Whiteness' as they are configured in terms of privatized feelings that are assessed through refractions of class, gender, sex, and generations, and that differently position white-, brown- and black-skinned people in terms of degrees of 'Whiteness': 'White' enough (or not), or too 'White'.[19]

A third point of interest in Ruth Kelly's speech relates to the limits of civility. Ruth Kelly's words conjure up a horizon of multicultural Britain that solidifies into white bodies that feel the proximity of diversity in various ways. These assumed generalized feelings become the justification for governing strategies aimed at the management and assurance of good feelings in what I refer to in Chapter 5 as 'feel-good politics' – but 'feel good' for whom? As I gesture towards in Chapters 2 to 4 and elaborate in Chapter 5, the once celebrated diversity becomes a source of discomfort that allows for white Britons to be uncivil towards those cast as the source of discomfort.

Feel-good politics are not new to multiculturalism. The inclusivist rhetoric of diversity of the late twentieth century packages diversity into a valuable asset to be managed and displayed for all to witness, consume, and find comfort in. In the Conservative government of 1990s Britain, if the project of multiculturalism virtually disappeared from the national political imaginary it still circulated in some local authorities as a feel-good, therapeutic, technology (Bhattacharyya 1998) aimed at diffusing racism and antagonistic views of difference. The celebration of diversity in the form of multicultural festivals seeks to show that the world can be a better place, that the world *is* a good place, 'if only we could see it' (Bhattacharyya 1998: 249). The typical strategy of this 'ludic multiculturalism' (Matuštík 1998) is to show people clothed in various 'ethnic' garb, serving 'ethnic' food to the tune of 'ethnic' or 'world' music with the dancers showcasing 'ethnic' steps in the background. People *embody* 'their "ethnic" culture, [in] a constant display of entertainment for others' (Bhattacharyya 1998: 259). This 'version of the translation of multiculturalism ... is the assertion that feeling good about your city [or nation] is about feeling comfortable with different people' (Bhattacharyya 1998: 258).

Multiculturalism as diffused diversity made its way into the British political horizon under Blair's New Labour government, and was initially the subject of the wide consensus that Ruth Kelly mentions. 'Diversity' was integral to Blair's project to 'modernize' Britain and to his agenda to establish Britain as a leading multicultural nation on the international stage. At the turn of the millennium, the Labour government declared its commitment to creating 'One Nation', a country where 'every colour is a good colour' and where 'racial diversity is celebrated.' (CFMEB 2000: 40).[20] In March 2000, the then Prime Minister Tony Blair declared that:

> This nation has been formed by a particularly rich complex of experiences: successive waves of invasion and immigration and trading partnerships, a potent mix of cultures and traditions which have flowed together to make us what we are today. Blood alone does not define our national identity. How can we separate out the Celtic, the Roman, the Saxon, the Norman, the Huguenot, the Jewish, the Asian and the Caribbean and all the other nations that have come and settled here? Why should we want to? It is precisely this rich mix that has made all of us what we are today.
>
> (Blair 2000)

Blair's list posits all groups on a system of equivalence, where all appear as ingredients that are added in equal proportion to the making of the 'rich mix' of the nation. There is no dominant group, here, no inequalities or discrimination. Moreover, Blair insists that differentiating between groups is unnecessary. 'Why should we want to' differentiate between them, he rhetorically asks. This vision for a 'new Britain' is one that 'doesn't see any broad civic value in the ability to live with difference' as Paul Gilroy states (2002). Rather, this vision is one that favours the transcendence of differences and dilution of oppositional politics in favour of an anonymized and universalized notion of 'diversity'. The nation here is an assumed bond where 'differences' are obliterated under a veneer of universal diversity – 'we are all different', 'we are all ethnics', 'we are all migrants', hence, 'we' are all the same.

'We like our diversity', Blair reiterated in December 2006. 'But how do we react when that "difference" leads to separation and alienation from the values that define what we hold in common?' Blair's diversity operates through difference-as-otherness for it is founded upon conditional inclusion/dilution. Diversity here is about the *achievement* of diluted differences for those worthy of it. The following chapters scrutinize the ways in which the 'rich' mix is selective about its components,[21] marking some 'differences' as soluble, others as indissoluble. What counts as 'diversity' and what counts as 'difference'? When does 'respectable diversity' (Bhattacharyya 1998) turn into unrespectable 'difference'? What kinds of mixing are acceptable, which are not? How is this written differently onto different bodies?

The mapping of multicultural Britain that this study offers concerns itself primarily with the national project and ideas of the nation/al which are already integral to multiculturalist politics. The following chapters document various incarnations of 'multicultural Britain' between 2000 and 2006 – not merely chronologically, but also simultaneously and contrapuntally. By this I mean that multiculturalism takes on various forms, not simply in succession, but also *simultaneously*, and their analysis allows us to understand 'multiculture' as a key site where the politics and culture of the nation and its limits are embattled. Thus rather than tracing a linear movement from multiculturalism to anti-multiculturalism and back again – as suggested by Ruth Kelly – I begin from the premise that the once-assumed clear division between multiculturalists (integrationists) and anti-multiculturalists (assimilationists) is now more blurred (Eller 1997) – if only at the level of all sharing a nationalist agenda where the preservation of the nation is 'ultimately and inevitably ... the backstop' (Mitchell 2004: 648). The question is, what national issues are at stake in celebrating, questioning, or dispensing with multiculturalism?

The book begins in October 2000, when the Commission on the Future of Multi-Ethnic Britain (CFMEB) published its report of the same title (CFMEB 2000). The furore surrounding the report – which is the subject of analysis in Chapter 2 – brought multiculturalism back to the centre of public debates. This resurgence is noteworthy not only because multiculturalism had become all but a dead letter as a government concern under the Conservative governments of the 1980s and 1990s, but because of how it recast multiculture *within* the nation. Cultural pluralism and ethnic diversification as a result of migration have been at the centre of the English and British 'identity crises' which have been so widely discussed in the public arena since the mid-twentieth century as to have become some of the most contested sites on the political landscape and in the cultural imagination.[22] With the publication of the 'Parekh Report', as the CFMEB report was also known, the debate moved on to the new ground of re-imagining Britain not only as a multicultural society or a multi-national state, but as a multicultural *nation* in the sense that Britishness is conceived as a unifying *identity* and *community* characterized by a long history of diversity and mixing that 'makes us what we are today', as Tony Blair put it in his 'Britain speech' cited above (Blair 2000).

Chapter 2 examines the role of emotions in distinguishing between legitimate and illegitimate patriotisms along the lines of pride and shame. The pride-shame debate reveals how the politics of pride seek to eradicate shame via an erasure of certain histories, and to sanitize Britishness under a veneer of tolerance. At the same time, multicultural tolerance necessitates the creation of intolerant culprits. Thus the chapter further uncovers the formation of new economies of exclusion/inclusion and toleration through different acts of interpellating 'others' to be *seen* to speak out as proud subjects of multicultural Britain. This leads to a broader argument about 'multiculturalist nationalism' and how 'multiculturalist citizenship' operates and comes about within it. Though it is widely assumed that neo-liberal citizenship is founded on conceptions of the disembodied subject, the chapter shows how particularized bodies are necessary to the multiculturalist project. Moreover, legitimacy operates differently on different bodies, and some minoritized subjects acquire legitimacy and the right to speak as citizens through a figurative peeling of skin that is imperative to the achievement of unmarked citizenship; imperative though impossible. This chapter, then, is about the skin of citizenship.

Chapter 2 shows how the very recognition of 'others' as legitimate, speaking subjects reconstitutes them as 'other' through a continuous process of de-racialization and re-racialization. Chapter 3 explores similar processes, but as they operate in representations of 'children of multicultural Britain' circulating in the national press between 2001 and 2006. 'Children of multicultural Britain' refers to those youths of minority ethnic or migrant parentage, some of mixed race parentage, some not, but who are all generalized as emblematic of multicultural Britain. This is about the multicultural youth as 'modal citizen' (Berlant 1997: 21) whose *form* is taken up repeatedly as the reflection, expression, promise, or threat of the changing nation/al. When considered together, the different Britains/Britons that the figurations bring forth – 'models of modern Britons' and 'monsters of modern Britain' – reveal the deep ambivalence of Britain's conception of 'the other within' who is expected to display not too much, not too little, but just enough alterity *of the right kind*. Drawing on photographic theory and psychoanalysis, I consider how representations of multicultural youths *simultaneously* embody the possibility of assimilation into, and destabilization of, Britain and Britishness. I argue that these figurations force the recognition of the very ambivalence of the nation/al as both *heimlich* and *unheimlich*, a thing of beauty and comfort, a thing of dread and death.

One issue considered in Chapter 3 is: what happens when 'they' become uncannily familiar? What happens when they appear so 'like us', but they turn out to be so 'unlike us'? In Chapter 4, I turn the question around: what happens when 'we' become like 'them'? The chapter revolves around a documentary produced for Channel 4 television and shown in October 2003, about the 'last white family' [sic] living in a working-class neighbourhood in Bradford in northern England, where the majority of residents are Pakistani and Bangladeshi Muslims. The film – entitled *The Last White Kids* (Thompson 2003) – taps into the fantasy nightmare of who 'we' might become if too exposed to minoritized subjects perceived as 'nonwhite' Britons. The personal and local forms of intimacy viewers were called upon to witness were making national culture a local affair, raising deep anxieties – expressed in press reviews of the film – over the future of Britain's children, but also of all Britons, in the portrayal of the excessive comfort of white working-class English girls with Islam, which was cast against the excessively violent discomfort of their brothers. More broadly, the chapter examines the *politics of interethnic propinquity* and how they are invested with particular ideals of good neighbourliness. By offering my own reading of *The Last White Kids* as a counterpoint to public imaginings of, and anxieties about, interethnic propinquity as they are conjured up and encoded in reviews of the film as well as in social policy guidelines, the analysis explores how the imperative of neighbourly love refers to both the desires for, and anxieties about, what multicultural intimacy stems from and fosters.

The chapters that follow variously explore the mutual constitution of particularism and universalism in the making of national community. Multicultural horizons are founded on privatized conceptions of multicultural citizenship, and their deployment as political imaginary combine conceptions of citizenship that are disembodied – the universalized, abstract/ed, a-cultural citizen – and embodied – where people in their ordinariness are the referent and where differences *are made (in)to* matter. In Chapter 5, I return to the question stated at the outset – how can we conceive of 'multiculture' in ways that address the complexities and intensities of feelings it invariably ignites? – and elaborate on the concept of multicultural intimacies to consider the economies of feelings that invest the concept and that the concept is invested in. Using a series of six vignettes depicting various encounters, I explore a range of feeling states that policy or popular representations and conceptions both produce and occlude by setting the discursive field within which the encounters depicted take place. Structured around two questions, 'how does it feel?' and 'how do you feel?', the vignettes describe felt encounters, bodily and emotive, that are animated and mediated through ideals of multicultural intimacy that circulate in the public domain. I consider how different feeling states are attributed different values – or rather, how they are differentially located within the 'national values' against which the 'value' of citizens is assessed. The next chapter, Chapter 2, begins this exploration in the analysis of exhortations of national pride.

2 Pride, shame, and the skin of citizenship

> Is it possible to reimagine Britain as a nation – a post-nation – in a multicultural way?
>
> (CFMEB 2000: 36)

In October 2000 in Britain, the publication of a report on the *Future of Multi-Ethnic Britain* (CFMEB 2000) triggered an intense debate that dominated the English press[1] for the subsequent four weeks. Against an outlook of impending change suggested by the report's title, a striking feature of the response to the report was the dominance of declarations that Britain and Britishness *are* and *always have been* inherently multicultural. As I explain below, such declarations were aimed at defying the report's suggestion that Britishness carries racial connotation, which was misread as an accusation of Britishness as inherently racist. The retort was clear: how can 'we' be racist if we've always been multicultural? 'We' are proud of 'our' *inherent* cultural diversity and recognize that it 'strengthens' and 'enriches' the nation.

This position dominated the response to the 'Parekh Report', as it is also known,[2] suggesting that the nation is perceived, almost unanimously, as impossible to conceive without *taking in* cultural minorities. This signalled a substantive shift in public understandings of what it means to be British today. Conceptions of Englishness as inherently multicultural, even hybrid, are not new (Palmer 2002), but this version of multicultural Britain shifts the focus away from Englishness towards a Britishness that is more than the cumulative effect of adding its constitutive parts (England, Scotland, Wales). This is a conception of Britishness that centres on ideas of inherent diversity and mixture that dissolve differences.[3] Mixing is a key principle of multicultural Britain, and is widely hailed as the antidote to segregation, differentialist politics, and the threats of racist violence and hate crimes. When couched in the language of kinship and bloodlines, the discourse of mixing serves to trace the genealogy of the nation's inherent hybridity and to recast diversity as a timeless characteristic of Britishness. 'We're all a little Brit of everything', as a *Daily Mirror* headline put it in October 2000, the author adding that '[g]enetically, the British are among the most multi-ethnic races on Earth' (Furbank 2000). As a 'nation of immigrants', in the words of the former Tory leader William Hague (Hague 2000), the Britain of the twenty-first century is one where the capacity to assimilate and absorb other cultures is celebrated. This contrasts with 1990s debates where concerns about immigration 'flows' presented the 'assimilation' of 'all other cultures' as forced upon Britain, and as a threat to 'our own identity' (*Daily Express* 31 May 1993, in Gabriel 1998: 104). Today, rather than seen as being forced *upon* Britain, assimilation is perceived as a force *of* Britishness (or Englishness, depending on who is speaking; see Ackroyd 2002).[4] That Britain is a 'Mongrel Nation'[5] is no longer a source of concern or shame, but rather of pride. This recasting of British history into a new genealogy of the British present is about *re-writing the national same so that 'we' could love ourselves as different.* Thus the hankering for national greatness endures, but its inflection differs from ideals of ethnic and racial homogeneity as they were articulated in Thatcher's and Major's 'back to basics' politics.

In October 2000, in the face of the inescapable 'multicultural question', as Stuart Hall puts it (2000), advocates of rightist, centrist, and leftist politics recognized that Britain is a multicultural society, and that, as 'a nation' it must take stock and contend with the presence of the 'other' within its midst. Britain, in this respect, is developing its own version of what I call 'multiculturalist nationalism', that is, the reworking of the nation as inherently multicultural.[6] Multiculturalism is generally considered in relation to specific national settings, but the predominant theory is that diversity is a disruptive, extraneous element causing a crisis of the nation, conceived as founded on monoculturalism. Similarly, 'multiculturalism' and 'nationalism' are widely conceived as relating to separate and distinct issues: the first with struggles over equality and recognition on the basis of 'identity politics'; the second, with politics of state sovereignty and exclusivity that are either associated with right-wing politics (such as the British National Party (BNP)) or with separatist movements (as in Quebec, the Basque country, or Northern Ireland). The question posed by the Parekh Report, and cited in the epigraph, resonates with such conceptions by suggesting that multiculturalism is post-national. In contrast, I suggest that in multiculturalist nationalism there is a shift away from linear narratives of nations moving *from* monoculture and exclusivity *to* multiculture and inclusivity, in favour of a narrative that posits multiculture and diversity at the heart of the nationalist project.

The media response to the Parekh Report suggested a version of British nationalism that imagines the nation as *already* inherently multicultural. A neo-ethnic version of national identity emerged: one based as a common hybridity. Gerd Baumann's remark about the US can be paraphrased here: 'It is the multiethnic hybridity of many [British] citizens that is used to argue for a shared neoethnic endorsement of national unity. If everyone's ancestry were "mixed", then everyone's present identity would be the same:

superethnically [British]' (1999: 34). Still primarily ethnicized, the new nation is now re-imagined as the result of a timeless mixing of cultures. This chapter is framed by a wider interest in what happens to the definition of 'national culture' when 'minority cultures' are not only let in, but redefined as *integral* to the nation itself (Ahmed 2000: 97). With respect to my immediate concerns, a further question is: *who* are the legitimate multicultural subjects entitled to belong to the national community and to speak in its name? In addition, what counts as a legitimate speech act?

I address these questions through the analysis of the pride politics that dominated the debate about the 'future of multi-ethnic Britain' in the four weeks following the release of the Parekh Report in October 2000; indeed, as I show below, the controversy was overshadowed by declarations of pride and accusations of shame. A key aim of this chapter is to consider the role of emotions – more specifically feelings for the nation – in policing the terms of belonging and entitlement to citizenry. By considering emotions as they are taken up and circulated in the press, I discuss the effects of displays of emotions on the kind of national community, and national subject, that are being imagined. What kinds of affective interpellation are being attempted in the deployment to the registers of pride and shame? In other words, how does the resort to the emotional registers of pride and shame position people in relation to each other, in relation to the nation, and to what it means to a 'good' patriotic citizen.

In psycho-sociology or in the sociology of emotions, shame is described as a deeply unsettling experience of the self that may occasion a withdrawal, a turning within oneself that is triggered by a perception of others' regard of oneself, of how one takes on the view of others as a judgment of one's moral character (Barbalet 2001; Katz 1999). Others, like Eve Sedgwick (2003) and Elspeth Probyn (2005), draw on the work of Silvan Tomkins (see Sedgwick and Frank 1995) to approach shame as a productive force; indeed, because it forces introspection and self-evaluation, shame can be transformative. What I take from these and others' scholarship is quite simple: that shame is both social and psychological and that it is fundamentally relational and formative.

In the case that is discussed here, shame is conceived as a threat to the national 'spirit'. It is about a feeling state that occurs when one – here, the nation – is being judged as unacceptable in some way. What interests me is how the perceived accusation of the nation and its history as being undesirable is refused and rejected through modes of deflecting shame onto the shamer, and of drawing pride back onto the national self. 'Shame and pride ... are different interlinings of the same glove', writes Eve Kosofsky Sedgwick (2003: 38). For Sedgwick, shame is 'theatrical performance' whereby '[p]erformance interlines shame as more than just its result or a way of warding it off, though importantly it is those things' (2003: 38). Sedgwick, following Tomkins, conceives shame as attaching itself to the sense of self, sharpening it and permanently transforming it. The implication is 'that one *is something* in experiencing shame' (Sedgwick 2003: 37; emphasis original). Refusal of shame is a refusal of the introspection, the self-evaluation that shame brings forth, and of the fragility that it brings about within the self (see Probyn 2005).

By tracing how shame is evoked, rejected, and projected onto particular subjects, I trace how shame is linked to the formation not only of 'self', but also of 'other', *within* the national collective. Thus I attend to the act of shaming – rather than to the experience of being shamed – as not only performance, but also as performative, that is as transformative of the national collective as a 'one' that should be proud and that should be the object of pride for its citizens. In doing so, the terms of inclusion distinguish those who are proud from those who are not and who are consequently shaming the nation. In this sense, pride is 'an entitlement', but not in the sense proposed by Probyn when she argues that 'pride politics' such as '[n]ational pride, black pride, gay pride, and now fat pride are all projects premised on the eradication of shame' (Probyn 2005: 2) and on the achievement of the state of pride once that eradication is complete. Pride, here, is rather an entitlement bestowed on those who display the right kind of pride and the right kind of refusal of shame. Pride and shame are indeed interlinings of the same glove that strikes or strokes: the glove that strikes you into shame and that one waves or wears with pride, or the glove that strokes you or shakes your hand in recognition of you 'doing us proud', as the English saying goes. The first section examines the role of shame and pride in distinguishing between legitimate and illegitimate patriotisms, that is, legitimate and illegitimate forms of attachment to the nation. The pride/ shame debate reveals how the politics of pride seek to eradicate shame via an erasure of certain histories, and to sanitize Britishness under a veneer of tolerance. In addition, the debate revolved around an anti-anti-racist argument that mobilized the multicultural as emblematic of the national character of inclusiveness and tolerance. At stake in such acts of shaming is the creation of intolerant culprits that are necessary for the maintenance of multicultural tolerance.

As I was studying the debates, questions of who spoke the multicultural 'we' and under what conditions also came increasingly to the fore. *Whose* emotions – whose pride in Britain – are being appealed to? How are they connected (or disconnected) to particular subjects? In the second section, the analysis centres on the formation of new economies of exclusion/ inclusion and toleration through different acts of calling upon 'others' to *be seen* to speak out as proud subjects of multicultural Britain. The very recognition of 'others' as legitimate speaking subjects forms those subjects in a particular way. Their declarations of pride function as personal testimonies, while at the same time the speakers are taken up as exemplary figures of multicultural, tolerant Britain. Their recognition as legitimate speaking citizens reconstitutes them as 'other' through a double process of de-racialization and re-racialization that operates through peeling the skin:

practices of unmarking the black skin, of making it disappear in the process of including proud black subjects within the national citizenry. In this respect, this chapter attends to the *skin of citizenship* and to the ways in which the politics of national multicultural pride variously and differentially enflesh its citizenry. More broadly, although focused on a very specific event, the material used here provides the basis for a wider examination of the mutual construction of particularism and universalism in the making of national community. The concluding section argues that 'multiculturalist citizenship' operates through a visual-oral economy that requires a process of ascription of differentiated identities, indeed of differentiated bodies, to some citizens by way of protecting the sanctity of the universal, invisible, and silent white British subject.

The politics of pride and shame

The Parekh Report was the result of the work of 'the Commission on the Future of Multi-Ethnic Britain', established in January 1998 by the Runnymede Trust, an independent think tank devoted to promoting racial justice. 'The Commission's remit was to analyse the current state of multi-ethnic Britain and to propose ways of countering racial discrimination and disadvantage' (CFMEB 2000: viii). The report's main intervention was in areas of social policy, offering extensive recommendations for policy developments in a range of areas, from policing though to education, the arts, and immigration, to name a few. This was an extensive and comprehensive document.[7] Yet the response to the report ignored all matters of social policy and instead focused on 'the report's questioning of the exclusionary implications of the category "British"' (Neal 2003: 60). Thus, when the 373-page report was released in October 2000, one short passage was the focus of much media attention:

> Britishness, as much as Englishness, has systematic, largely unspoken, racial connotations. Whiteness nowhere features as an explicit condition of being British, but it is widely understood that Englishness, and therefore by extension Britishness, is racially coded ... Unless these deep-rooted antagonisms to racial and cultural difference can be defeated in practice, as well as symbolically written out of the national story, the idea of a multicultural post-nation remains an empty promise.
> (CFMEB 2000: 38–39)

Because of its association with white supremacy, white privilege, imperialism, and its historical position at the centre of British political and cultural life, the Parekh Report rejects Englishness as an appropriate label for the re-imagined multi-ethnic nation. In turn, it reluctantly takes on Britishness as the best available term to designate the common terrain of belonging that 'communities' share. 'Britishness is not ideal', the report states, 'but at least it appears acceptable, particularly when suitably qualified – black British, Indian British, British Muslim, and so on' (CFMEB 2000: 38).

This was received with a wave of criticism from some sections of the English press,[8] and was taken as an unwarranted accusation of racism. 'British is racist, says peer trying to rewrite our history' (Irwin and Hughes 2000); 'Racism slur on the word "British"' (Doughty 2000a). Missing the nuance between 'racial connotations' and 'racism', journalists consistently misrepresented and misquoted the Report as rendering 'British' *inherently* racist (as opposed to historically racist). For Sarah Neal, this hostile response 'provides a recent example of the longevity of an anti-anti-racism discourse' in the media, and its tendency to derive the 'newsworthiness' of racial equality policies 'from their potential to be either ridiculed or presented as a threat to national identity' (Neal 2003: 60). This discourse operates through a rejection of any recognition of the place of racism – or of 'race' and racial hierarchy – in the historical process of state formation and nation-building.

In accordance with this anti-anti-racist view, equally controversial was the report's claim that the 'national story' should be rethought and reworked, with certain aspects perhaps jettisoned, if the story is to produce a new collective self-image that would be 'more flexible, inclusive, cosmopolitan' (CFMEB 2000: 15). The report rightly calls for a politics of reckoning with the imperial past, which it claims will be achieved through the difficult task of:

> expunging the traces of an imperial mentality from the national culture, particularly those that involved seeing the white British as a superior race … This mentality penetrated everyday life, popular culture and consciousness. It remains active in projected fantasies and fears about difference, and in racialised stereotypes of otherness. The unstated assumption remains that Britishness and whiteness go together, like roast beef and Yorkshire pudding … The absence from the national curriculum of a rewritten history of Britain as an imperial force, involving dominance in Ireland as well as in Africa, the Caribbean and Asia, is proving from this perspective to be an unmitigated disaster.
>
> (CFMEB 2000: 24–25)

The Parekh Report was calling for an acknowledgment of the historical legacies of imperialism in the constitution of a racially connoted idea of Britishness, as well as in shaping present conditions of racism within broader social relations and social inequalities. Implicit in this proposal was the acknowledgement that we are not only subjects of history, but also agents of history – revisiting the past might allow for the creation of different futures. But critics were quick to seize this and see it as an 'assault on national pride' (Irwin and Hughes 2000), a 'promot[ion of] national guilt', a 'brainwashing exercise designed to destroy our sense of nationhood' (P.

Johnson 2000), an 'attempt to destroy our centuries-old culture' (Clarkson 2000), and 'to rewrite our history' (Johnston 2000). In response, they endeavoured to recover the glories of British history, and its numerous achievements. Boadicea, the Magna Carta, the abolitionist movement, Waterloo, VE Day: these events were indiscriminately listed and hailed as evidence of the enduring British values of fairness, resilience, tolerance, democracy, and decency. History, with a capital H, was seen to be brought to trial – accused of racism – and many were queuing up to defend it.

One of the challenges in facing up to the past lies in the tension between acknowledgment/interpretations of the past, on the one hand, and accountability/self-examination for social relations in the present, on the other. The Parekh Report's call to revise the national story, as well as the outcry that this triggered, were *both* wedded to the project of asserting a 'new' Britain, but with different ways of relating to the 'old' one. What is the role of the 'new' as a way of writing history? What is it that people are trying to recover, forget, or erase? What is at stake in refusing to acknowledge the terrors of the past? In their aspiration to be 'truly multicultural', politicians and sections of the English press refused the idea that British subjects could be 'shamed by past imperial, colonial, and racist attitudes that are now understood as having ... constituted' (Povinelli 2002: 18) the dark side of the nation's history. Elizabeth Povinelli shows how, in Australia, statespeople represent *themselves* and the nation as such shamed subjects and in that context 'multiculturalism is represented as the externalized political testament to the nation's aversions to its past misdeeds, and to its recovered good intentions' (2002: 18). Povinelli is writing about how an Australian national identity is claimed through shame which, as Sara Ahmed documents, works 'to acknowledge past wrongdoings, whilst absolving individuals from guilt' (2004: 101). In Britain, in contrast, neither the Parekh Report nor its detractors were calling for a collective moment of shame in a cleansing process of recovery and recognition of its past misdeeds. The report was appealing to a sense of history that acknowledges the role of imperialism, white supremacy, and racial thought in the forging of present day Britain and Britishness. But critics of the report were quick to interpret this as an unacceptable act of shaming, and in response, multiculture was mobilized as a testament to Britain's glories and non-racist past. The public outcry against the report evacuated questions of history and reckoning with the past, and instead centred on the search for, and prosecution of, those who might be held accountable for what was perceived as a generalized loss of pride and patriotism among Britons. The report was thus seen as part of a wider problem. The question of pride and patriotism dominated much of the debate, which was marked by mutual blaming and shaming in a tug of war over who held the highest patriotic moral ground.

At one end, conservative rightists accused Lord Parekh and the commissioners of the report, along with the Labour government, the chattering classes and the 'Islingtonian intelligentsia',[9] for being 'ashamed of our history and feel[ing] the need to apologise' (*Sun* leading article 12 October 2000). At the other end, Jack Straw, then Home Office Secretary, reacted by distancing himself and the government from the Parekh Report in the face of criticism that he and his Labour colleagues were unpatriotically ashamed of being British. 'I am proud to be English and proud to be British', he declared. 'I am proud of what I believe to be the best of British values.' And he added: 'Unlike the Runnymede Trust, I firmly believe that there is a future for Britain and a future for Britishness' (in Ford 2000). He later joined the collective admonition of blame by pointing the accusative finger for lack of patriotism to the political left: 'Given the Left's tendency to wash their hands of the notion of nationhood', he wrote in the *Observer*, 'it's unsurprising our perception of Britishness became a conservative one' (Straw 2000).[10]

Pride in Britishness became a resonating mantra that rang through the arguments against the recommendations of the Parekh Report that Britain should rethink its 'national story' and identity. Letters and articles followed each other in claiming love and pride in Britain, and disclaiming any shame or guilt whatsoever: 'I am a Sri Lankan Tamil who came here 30 years ago. I show my British passport with pride, not shame' (Chandran 2000); 'In Sydney [the Sydney Olympics of 2000] it felt great being British, and that should never be taken away … to compete for your country is about taking pride in where you come from' (Simon Dennis, Olympic gold medallist in the British men's eight rowing team, in Hume 2000); 'I'm proud to be British and call myself British. If you're not proud to be British then you're living in the wrong place' (Craig David, musician, in Doughty 2000b); 'I am proud to be British. I have done well by being in Britain. We are still the country that everybody respects' (Sarwar Ahmed, 'millionaire media magnate' [sic], in Doughty 2000b); 'I am proud of being British. I have no guilt about it' (Lord Paul (Swraj Paul), Labour life peer, in Laville 2000).

Running through these exhortations of pride is one refrain: the repelling of shame and national guilt. The politics of pride deployed in response to the Parekh Report seek to eradicate shame; pride in 'our' history, in 'our' country, in 'our' passports, is repeatedly rehearsed by way of sanitizing the attachment to the nation under a veneer of guiltless pride, one which knows no shame or guilt. It is noteworthy that shame and guilt are somehow conflated here; that the attacks on Lord Parekh and his co-commissioners treat shame and guilt equally: as repulsive, unwanted, and illegitimate affects to be eradicated from the collective body.[11] This conflation is indicative of the ambivalence that Paul Gilroy picks up on when he writes of Britain's post-colonial melancholia; that is, the distress caused by the realization of the empire's violence and abuses, while there is also a desire to remember the empire as a source of national pride and accomplishment, and as a key site of identification. Gilroy wonders how 'British political culture has had to adapt in order to make sense of the catalogue of horror that extends into the present' and proposes to consider 'the political and psychological reactions which attend to the discovery that imperial administration was ... necessarily a violent, dirty, and immoral business. We need to know how that deeply disturbing realization *has been managed*' (2004a: 102; emphasis added). The focus of Gilroy's attention are the strategies deployed to deal with Britain's 'guilt-ridden loathing' (2004a: 98), and so he unpacks recent revisions and reassessments of British history (such as Colley 2003) that defensively minimize the Empire along with its brutal character, and aggrandize 'the British themselves [as] the ultimate tragic victims of their extraordinary imperial success' (2004a: 103). In contrast, the management strategies deployed in the row over the Parekh Report seek to subsume Britain's violent and bloody imperial past into a revision of the national story that embellishes the national 'we' as inherently tolerant and welcoming to others. No room for aggrandized victimization here; rather than 'guilt-ridden', this is a show of a proud and 'guilt-free look' at British history and at what is euphemistically referred to as the 'oddities of imperialism' (G. Johnson 2002).

Some theorists, such as Axel Honneth (1992) or Elspeth Probyn (2000, 2005) have discussed how the repelling of shame is about self-affirmation whereby the once shamed subject/body is now declaring its self-pride – for example in lesbian/gay/bisexual/transgender pride, or fat pride (Probyn 2000: Chapter 6). But here, in contrast, the repelling of shame is a *refusal* to make it 'ours' in the first place, a refusal to interiorize it in the national body, a refusal to consider that shame might be a feature of the attachment to the nation, or, as in Australia, a feature of the nation's past (Ahmed 2004; Povinelli 2002). Shame is not evoked as something the national 'we' no longer wants to feel, or something that 'we' recognize so that 'we' can feel better. It is not even put up as a choice against the valorization of the past (Hage 2003: 4–5). Shame, here, is rejected outright as something that the national 'we' has not internalized in the first place – and indeed that should not be internalized full stop. Shame, here, is exteriorized, rejected, pushed out, and projected onto those who are guilty of unpatriotic feelings or acts. Shame is replaced by anger expressed against 'them' who are seen as being ashamed of 'us'-the-nation, and against 'them' who shame 'us'-the-nation. Invested in the process of eradicating shame from the collective body is, paradoxically, a process of splitting the national collective between patriots and unpatriotic culprits. The latter includes two figures: the dissenter and the hooligan.

First, the dissenter who is the 'unpatriotic' liberal and leftist who questions the national story and the notion of a historically fair, just and inclusive Britain. The culprit here is accused of being at the source of a dwindling pride in the nation; the condemned act: expressing dissent or attempting to criticize the national state, and suggesting ways for redress and consistency – for example the Parekh Report's suggestion for a revision of the national story. Such acts are deemed as threats to the duty of patriotic citizenship, a duty that is primarily a collective duty, that is, a duty to the national community. As Paul Gilroy suggests, '[t]his state of affairs is alarming because it represents the erasure either of any positive sense of the value of dissent or of necessary distance from the national culture's imaginary centre of gravity. It scorns the idea that dissidence should be a measure of the buoyancy and health of democracy' (2003: 266). By turning dissent into a shameful act, the very possibility of think- ing of dissent not only as a democratic act, but as an act of national attachment, is undermined.

In addition, as explained above, the scorn against the unpatriotic dis- sident is also about the maintenance of a guilt-free national story. The Parekh Report's recommendation to rewrite the national story of Britain as an imperial force was rejected by critics as 'promot[ing] national guilt' (P. Johnson 2000). Reckoning with the history of racism – that is, reckoning with Britain as *historically* racist – could potentially clear a space for the expression of anger by many of Britain's citizens. What is threatening to the white subject, as Gunaratnam and Lewis (2001) suggest, is the black subject's anger. The shame of white people's history of racism is averted through anger against those subjects, white or black, whose own anger is threatening to effect 'white guilt' (Gunaratnam and Lewis 2001: 143). Thus we could begin to make sense of the predominance of black faces that were seen to declare their pride in Britishness in October 2000. The refusal of shame is also about the anger of black subjects. (I return to the hailing of ethnic minorities in the next section.)

The positions alluded to above (the angry black subject and the shamed white subject) are not complete or static. But in the press debates around the Parekh Report, the rejection of shame was inextricably related to the rejection of perceived accusations of racism. A sanitized, happy multi- culturalism requires the eradication of unwanted unhappy subjects, including those whose anger might be justified but which can be managed and redirected away from the nation (the collective self) and onto indivi- dualized selves. Thus, a second unpatriotic culprit hovered in the back- ground of the pride/shame debate: the intolerant racist thug, emblematically represented by the flag-waving white BNP-activist's 'ugly face of patriotism' (Travis 2000). This figure was more often explicitly invoked by politicians themselves, rather than journalists or other com- mentators. In the midst of the 'patriotism tug-of-war' mentioned above, Jack Straw felt compelled to urge the British left 'not [to] leave patriotism to [the] far right' (in Travis 2000), and to 'reclaim national pride from racists and xenophobic football thugs' (Irwin and Hughes 2000). Thus the pride/shame debate was in part a struggle between political parties[12] over who lays claims to 'real patriotism' and, crucially, to the right to 'author' the nation. But the same shameful figure of the 'racist thug' haunted those commentators who repeatedly rejected the Parekh Report's statement about the racial connotations of Britishness. Though racism was recognized by some as part of British life and institutions, the general outcry was against the perceived accusation that the British people are racists. Being British is *not* being racist, we were insistently told, because 'we' are tolerant and have welcomed and absorbed migrants and their cultures for centuries. As Robin Wiegman has noted, the well-intentioned liberalist turn towards tolerance, inclusion, and diversity is characterized by a disaffiliation from the more overt forms of racism and racial violence (in Chow 2002: 13), associated here with the white working-class BNP-activist or football hooligan. The darker side of history is evacuated by ascribing the origins and sources of racism and intolerance to individuals, to singular figures, or within specific localities and sub-cultures. The shameful subjects, the bad citizens, the racists, are held solely accountable for hate crimes. Exhortations of pride project shame onto outcast subjects who are a source of revulsion for the 'decent majority'. They, the racists, are the source of 'our' shame: the meanings of shame are seen to *originate* from, and *reside* in, the actions of these subjects. Conversely, the placement of shame and guilt on individual bodies allows for the nation and its 'decent majority' to emerge as naturally tolerant and inclusive. Wider questions of collective accountability and self-examination are concealed, indeed evacuated, in the creation of injurious subjects (Butler 1997).

In sum, the repeated declarations and displays of pride simultaneously produce the subjects of shame – those who are ashamed as well as those who are 'our' shame – and the subjects of pride – the 'proud' subjects and the subjects of 'our' collective pride in 'our' inclusive multiculturality. At the same time, while the eradication of shame pushes the dissident or racist subject outside of the national community, it also differentiates between citizens along racialized identities. The effect of the politics of pride is to separate ethnic 'others' into subjects who must be hailed as figures of the tolerant, multiracial Britain that many commentators 'cherish'. They constitute 'our' diversity, which is what 'we' are proud of. A new visual referent of what it means to be British is surfacing from the debate; a particular 'vision' of who 'we' are that relies on the 'other' in a way that reconstitutes and reinvests the privileges of whiteness in a different way (Wiegman in Chow 2002: 13): through a cathectic investment in multiculture-as-tolerance evidenced by the racially-minoritized subject speaking his or her pride in the nation.

The vision and skin of multicultural Britain

A striking feature of the pride politics deployed in response to the Parekh Report is the compulsion to testify; the compulsion to publicly declare oneself as a proud Briton; the compulsion to 'speak out' and to *be seen* to be a proud Briton. The pride politics, in this respect, are telling enactments of the liberal faith in the intentional subject. As Lauren Berlant (2001) argues, testimony plays a crucial role in supporting a neo-liberal agenda based on the construction of the voluntaristic, individual, and individuated self. This is particularly relevant to the case examined here, where the declarations are deployed in the form of the personal testimony, and addressed in the form of the public letter. What is the relationship between the 'I' who speaks, and the 'we' it simultaneously speaks with, to, and of? How does the 'I' – the individual, particularized body – relate to the collective 'we' – the national body, the collective mass identification – in textual and visual displays of the self-declared proud Briton?

One good example is Kelly Holmes's declaration. Then a bronze medallist in the Sydney Olympics,[13] Holmes's statement appeared in the *Daily Mail* next to the standard photograph of the black athlete wrapped in the Union Jack.

> I'm proud of being British. I served in the Army for nine-and-a-half years as a Sergeant PT instructor and I never had any problems regarding race. If you're born in Britain, and your parents are British and you live here, then you're British it doesn't matter what colour you are. I don't understand what the issue is.
>
> (in Doughty 2000b)

In a highly significant move, Holmes declares that 'one' is British no matter what colour she is. Her refusal to identify as 'black' is a refusal of the primacy of skin colour and racial identification. Refusing to be forced to identify racially, Holmes is stating that what matters is individual history rather than skin colour, thus precisely undermining the very subject position she is called upon to occupy: the black British *other*.

Holmes's refusal can be read as effecting a kind of deracination – not from 'roots', but from the historical conditions that 'other' her skin colour; that is, that have rendered her skin colour the constitutive other of Britishness. However, what interests me here is how Holmes's and others' declarations were taken up by the English press. Despite her refusal of blackness, Holmes (and others) circulated within an iconography of Britishness that put skin colour at the *forefront* of the meaning of Britishness. The way she and others were taken up by the press was *as* racialized subjects. Yet significantly, their dark skins were gradually peeled off in the process of making them British. David Green, director of *Civitas*, a rightist independent think-tank, carried out an act of peeling the skin when he stated in the *Daily Mail* that:

> When I saw Denise Lewis and Audley Harrison speaking at the Olympics I was taking less and less notice of their skin colour and more and more of the fact that what they were saying was full of British attitudes. They were praising their families and talking about hard work. What is important for many people is less their ethnic origin than the fact of being raised in Britain.
>
> (in Doughty 2000a)

The gradual erasure of the skin moves along the gradual recognition that Lewis and Harrison are 'like us', underneath. Lewis, Harrison, and Holmes are the legitimate 'familiar others', to paraphrase Sara Ahmed (2000: 106–7). Their skin is shed so they can reveal their true colour(s): displaying the right attitude and uttering and *doing* the right things – wave the Union Jack, join the British Army, praise family values, sanction the work ethic – thus making them eligible for incorporation within the 'welcoming' nation, who in turn can claim its own distinctiveness as a tolerant and inclusive society. The authenticating black voice of the individual success story is cited as evidence of the opportunities offered to all (Gabriel 1998: 77).

The testimonies that arose against the Parekh Report were at once individual and impersonal: they operated as a form of self-expression while supporting the belief in the irrelevance of individual difference for contemporary British citizenship, as long as individuals express pride in British values and support for its institutions. As they talk, they become more British; talk produces British flesh. Inherent in the declarations of pride is an utter faith in the transparency of discursive utterances. Talking the talk of national allegiance and pride makes the 'other' one of 'us' and the non-white skin colour is rendered irrelevant. Their deracination makes them available to adopt 'the nation' and available for adoption by 'the nation'.[14] It is worth noting that the fact that Holmes, Lewis, and Harrison were hailed in the first place is a familiar instance of the celebrated sportsperson who is adopted by the nation because of his or her refusal to identify as black or to talk about racism (Carrington 2000).

Within liberal multiculturalist conceptions of citizenship, there is an uninterrogated assumption that *any* body, insofar as they 'enter into the bargain of intelligibility' (Berlant 2001: 49–50) – that is, to put it simply, that they speak the right language and do the right thing – has unproblematic access to citizenship and legal/legitimate personhood. But what theories of liberal citizenship gloss over is the process of ascription of differential identities, and indeed of differential bodies, to some citizens rather than others within multiculturalist nationalism. Within the vision of British tolerance and 'rich mix', there is an assumed freedom, movement, and choice, offered to British citizens. One which allows, indeed prescribes, a detachment from some ethnic identifications and differences in favour of the attachment to an idealized abstract post-ethnic *British* citizen. The interpellation of ethnic minorities to declare their Britishness via values and allegiance is a call to an ethnic dis/identification as unqualified British – that is, with no black, Asian, or any other 'ethnic' qualifier.[15] However, a tension arises between the idealized moment of abstraction, on the one hand, and the place of the embodied 'other', on the other. What happens when speech is *not* separated from the body (Berlant 2001), but rather (re)connected to particular bodies? How can we account for the fact that, in the pride politics displayed in October 2000, the visual representation of the 'beautiful face of patriotism' (as opposed to the 'ugly face of patriotism' cited earlier) was figured predominantly, if not exclusively, in photographs of people of colour? What does it mean to call upon particular bodies to be seen to declare their allegiance to Britishness? Whose voices are being hailed and whose bodies are being seen to speak are not left to chance. The successful black bodies seen to declare their pride in Britain were inscribed with dignity, lawfulness, and personal achievement, as they were heard to subscribe to the universalized values of Britishness.

Deployed as counternarratives to the perceived accusation of Britishness as racist, these declarations of pride are cast as evidence that Britain and Britishness are not racist, that Britain is in fact a great place to *be* 'ethnic' – 'this is a good country in which to be a member of an ethnic minority' (Chandran 2000). Newspaper editors and journalists called upon members of ethnic minorities to speak out and be seen as proud Britons. The use of their declarations within the context of the public outcry against a presumed attack on national tolerance and national pride re-racializes the speakers in a particular way. These individuals were hailed as already recognized, legitimate speaking subjects. But as Sara Ahmed points out: '[h]ailing as a form of recognition which constitutes the subject it recognises ... might function to differentiate *between* subjects, for example, by hailing differently those who seem to belong and those who might already be assigned a place – out of place – as "suspect"' (2000: 23). In other words, black and Asian Britons were 'hailed' in the Althusserian sense of being called upon to be accountable, to declare their attachment to Britain, and to silence any anger or dissent, whereby they will be recognized as legitimate subjects. However, the very act of hailing 'them' *as* 'ethnic' – which in Britain still means 'immigrant' and 'non-white' – also produces them as already suspect of *dis*-identification. Consequently, the very identities of 'black-British' or 'Asian-British', which the declarations of pride sought to consolidate, are instead rendered indeterminate. As wilful subjects – 'The truth is that *nobody forced me* or any other immigrant to become British. *I did so by choice*' (Chandran 2000; emphasis added) – who are still 'recognized' as other, their allegiance to the nation is something to be achieved and repeatedly tested. Indeed, their hailing in October 2000 can be seen as a prelude to the mediatic hailing of British Muslims after 11 September 2001, who were repeatedly required to testify their allegiance to Britain, their condemnation of the attacks in the US in September 2001, *and* their support of the bombing of Afghanistan. Later, in the context of the US/UK alliance in the war on Iraq, British Muslims were called upon to support the British government and, similarly, following 7 July 2005, British Muslims were further called upon not only to condemn the attacks in London, but to disidentify with the attackers and with any version of Islam that may condone such acts. These examples illustrate how in the British politics of multiculturalism, minorities' ethnicity is understood as otherness, foreignness from 'mainstream' British culture (some more than others), but is also part of a relation of cultural politics where it is assumed that they can transact their ethnicity and culture, and where their ethnicity can be shed or exchanged for legitimate citizenship. In order to be welcome in the national fold, they must deracinate themselves, yet they remain, willingly or not, aligned to their ethnic otherness.

Thus, while these proud faces of new multiculturalist Britain comfort the nation in its claims to be a model of multiculturalism, it is their very 'difference' that marks them as alien, even as potential 'enemy aliens'. In a context where the possibility of *dis*identification, or ambivalent forms of connections with 'being British' are insistently foreclosed, it is those who must *acquire* the right to dwell and the status of legitimate personhood and citizenship, who are called upon to be seen to testify their allegiance. The 'voluntary' embrace of Britishness by those who have historically been its constitutive outside does not necessarily guarantee their seamless and unquestioned inclusion within the political signifier. For they are always suspected of being more saturated by their ethnicity, culture, or religion, than the white British citizen is.

The visual–oral economy of multiculturalist citizenship

The formation of multicultural citizenry involves a movement between closeness and distance; that is, one which means that the minoritized ethnic other is now integral to the national imagined community, while at the same time their otherness, which is necessary to the project of multiculturalist Britain, keeps them distant and indeterminate. At a time when being a good Briton equals being a proud Briton, when political factions are fighting over the laurels of patriotism, and when the perceived issue at stake is the nation's multicultural tolerance past and present, *all* citizens, but especially minorities, are expected to reiterate their allegiance to Britishness and their pride in the nation. In this context, the repeated acts of hailing 'multicultural subjects' simultaneously produce them as undeniably 'different' and 'the same' at the same time. For instance, hailing 'visible minorities' (Marr 2000a: 154) as speaking, voluntaristic selves simultaneously produces them as wilful subjects, thus opening up the possibility of ambivalent attachments to the nation, expressed in dissent, anger, or refusal. Hence the debate around the Parekh Report was connected to a political rhetoric of citizenship that assumes sameness between individuals by denying the socio-political significance of 'difference' and evacuating histories of domination, racism, and resistance.

In contrast to theories of liberal citizenship that assume that the legitimate subject-citizen is a disembodied subject, this chapter suggests that 'multiculturalist citizenship' requires a process of ascription of differentiated identities and of differentiated bodies to its citizens. Multiculturalist citizenship oscillates between conceptions founded on the *embodied* multicultural – where people in their ordinariness are the referent – and the *disembodied* citizen or community – the utopian moment of abstraction, where the nation is an assumed bond, an imagined community of shared allegiance where 'differences' are transcended at the level of action and of citizenship. The debates around the Parekh Report marked a shift into a reconstitution of the deep intertwining of the universal and the particular, where particularized citizenship is a necessary condition to the maintenance of the universal point of reference. Feminist and post-colonial scholarship (Alexander and Mohanty 1997; Bhabha 1994; Chakrabarty 2000; Chatterjee 1986, 1993; Hesse 1999) has precisely shown how the universal is always configured around the containment and disavowal of particularized bodies. But in the making of a 'new Britain' that is inherently multicultural, there is a new inflection to this relation precisely through the skin of citizenship that not only contains particularized bodies within the borders of the state, but that also allows for some subjects to momentarily renegotiate their position within the citizenry in an imperative exchange of ethnicities from the minoritized to the national. Indeed, what characterizes the debates around the Parekh Report is that the bodies of some were de-marked, or un-marked, showing how *conceptions* of difference *are* alterable, *can* be unfixed, and are always negotiable – though not on a level playing-field. By extension, the relationship between the universal and the particular is not fixed; it is not equated to the one between the disembodied white national and the embodied non-white. It is also one that is integral to a politics of citizenship where minoritized subjects themselves must be disciplined into programmatic structures of engaged citizenship and political participation that rely on feelings for the nation, on expressions of emotional presence and commitment, and on a detachment from 'roots' that erases certain histories in favour of others. Concealed in the process is the enfleshment of citizenship as white-bodied.

Multiculturalist nationalism entails shifting the mechanics of creating national communities by presenting new national family portraits that suggest a substantive shift in who 'we' are. In a mimetic relationship between representation and identity, the assumption is that if the visual referent changes, 'we' change, and that consequently disenfranchised communities will be satisfied as a result of feeling greater pride in being part of the national community by virtue of seeing 'fellow members' of 'their' communities within the representational field (Phelan 1993: 7). British multiculturalist nationalism reflects what Peggy Phelan calls 'the ideology of the visible, an ideology which erases the power of the unmarked, unspoken, unseen' (Phelan 1993: 7). The ideology of the visible rests on the presumption that identities are visibly marked so that those sharing physical resemblances will align themselves to a same community. A second presumption is that 'increased visibility equals increased power' (Phelan 1993: 7). But whose power is this about? As stated earlier, talking the talk and walking the walk of national allegiance makes the 'other' one of 'us' and the non-white skin colour is peeled off, *rendered irrelevant.*

Called upon as racially-marked subjects, they must be *un*-marked if the promise of the national bond is to be sustained. The empowered are not the disenfranchized, but the nation and its 'decent' unmarked citizens, whose integrity and privilege remain cloaked under the mantle of 'universal' values: tolerance, fair play, and the freedom and choice of allegiance. Entitlement to national citizenry is about choosing to ignore the concealed markings of 'race', as well as class (remember the 'ugly face of patriotism'; more on class in the following chapters), and the very historical conditions that have brought some citizens to speak as 'other' in the first place. While minorities are aligned to visible 'communities', it is the coherence and strength of the wider national community that is ultimately re-asserted. Paraphrasing Ahmed (2000: 173), the displays of pride speak of a universal national 'we' by translating how 'they' proudly live *here* into a 'we' that speaks 'our' national pride.

The impetus in foregrounding the other within the new family portrait is not so much to defend the integrity of cultural difference, but rather to preserve the sanctity of the universal, which is deeply wedded to the power of an unmarked whiteness. If the formless national subject is formless by virtue of it being unmarked, the process of unmarking operates differently on different bodies. The disembodied silent subject is the one who has the right to dwell in the first place, and whose attachment to the nation goes unquestioned: the white Briton. The embodied multicultural subject achieves unmarked status through the injunction to speak his and her allegiance and pride in the nation/al. One must be *seen* and *heard* to declare her pride in Britishness in order to *achieve* un-marked status – an 'achievement' that is endlessly deferred, as the non-white skin is never fully peeled off, in a continuous process of de/re-racialization. As stated earlier, ethnicity here is conceived as foreignness and otherness, but it is also seen as something that one can willingly shed in exchange for legitimate citizenship. In multiculturalist Britain, conceptions of the universal formless citizen are in tension with the ascription of embodied and particularized 'otherness' to ethnic minorities, who must *stay in place as 'other'* in order to claim the *multi* of multiculturalism. In the process, Britishness-as-Whiteness – that is, as *both* a property of Britishness and a regime of looking (Seshadri-Crooks 2000; see Chapter 1) – is re-naturalized through the re-affirmation of the legitimacy and belonging of the unmarked subjects. In the multiculturalist public sphere, speech is more legitimate as it becomes more attached to some bodies and detached from others.

3   'Children of multicultural Britain'
The good, the bad, the uncanny

In one sense at least, and in spite of the massive difference in the number of deaths, British society was more deeply traumatised by the two London attacks bombings [sic] than Americans were in the aftermath of 9/11. The United States assailants were foreigners; the eight people involved in London were the children of Britain's own multicultural society.

(Kepel 2005)

And the person or thing photographed is the target ... which I would like to call the *Spectrum* of the Photograph, because this word retains, through its root, a relation to 'spectacle' and adds to it that rather terrible thing which is there in every photograph: the return of the dead.

(Barthes 1981: 9)

Meet '[t]he face of Britain' (Anonymous 2001; Hartley 2001). Or, as another source put it, 'Meet the population of Britain' (S. Millar 2001). The 'Face of Britain' (see Figure 3.1) was produced by Chris Dorley-Brown from the portraits of 1,900 residents of Haverhill (Suffolk), male and female, aged six-months-old to eighty-years-old, allegedly including 'representatives of about 50 ethnic minorities, showing the cultural diversity of the town' (in Anonymous 2001).[1] The 1,900 photographs were digitally merged to create what has been perceived as the 'average 21st century Briton' (S. Millar 2001). 'Although it is taken from a snapshot of people in the town of Haverhill', said Dorley-Brown, 'it could really represent the face of the average person in Britain' (Anonymous 2001). What does making this composite image of 1,900 residents of a small town in Suffolk (South East England) into a national portrait tell us about the fantasy of the national self?[2] I began collecting more images. On the bulletin board and wall facing my desk, and on my computer hard drive, are press cuttings, postcards, downloaded and scanned images, all featuring different 'faces of multicultural Britain'. This collection is a telling sample of

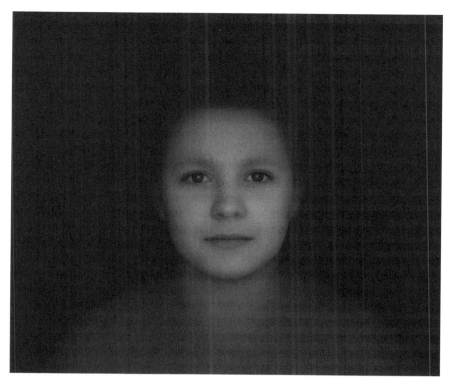

Figure 3.1 *'The Face of Britain', or 'Haverhill 2000'.* Courtesy of Chris Dorley-Brown & Haverhill Town Council.

different imagined phenotypes of 'new' Britishness – the faces of Britain – that circulate in the public domain, and that have been offered up as emblematic of utopian or dystopian visions of multiculture: from 'models of modern Britons' to the monstrous 'children of multicultural Britain'.

This chapter examines the figure of 'multicultural youth' as it circulated in various forms in the British national press between 2001 and 2006. 'Multicultural youth' refers not only to the child of 'mixed race' parentage, but also to the young person whose cultural referents originate from a range of sources and places – the cultural 'hybrid'. Though there is an extensive literature on 'mixed race' and 'hybrid' youth cultures in Britain and elsewhere, attention is not paid to the ways in which the figure of the 'mixed', 'hybrid', or 'multicultural' youth is integrated within the fantasy structures of the nation. The chapter title borrows the phrase 'children of multicultural Britain' from Gilles Kepel (cited in the first epigraph) because it captures this kind of deployment within the national fantasy. Kepel was not alone in conceiving the suicide-bombers of July 2005 as the failed offspring of state multicultural policies and practices – as the nation's children. This image widely circulated in several sections of the press in the days following the tragic events of 7/7. Expanding on the notion of 'children of multicultural Britain', this chapter considers the ways in which the nation's value, achievements, and future horizons are figured 'not on behalf of an actually existing and laboring adult', to paraphrase Lauren Berlant, but on behalf of the not-yet fully formed citizen, 'of a future [Briton], both incipient and pre-historical: especially invested with this hope [is] the [British youth]' (1997: 6).[3]

Children began to figure prominently by the end of New Labour's first term in office (1997–2001) and Labour's manifesto for the general election of 2001 featured a host of child-focused policies and 'was rife with pictures of children' (Dobrowolsky 2002: 44). In the aftermath of the riots of 2001 in three towns in northern England, the figure of minoritized youth as doubly disaffected because they were 'caught between two cultures', as the catchphrase goes, dominated Home Office documents about community cohesion that sought ways to avoid future racial conflicts by proposing 'mixing' as the path towards harmonious community relations (Home Office 2001a and b; see Chapter 4). Subsequent Home Office documents make 'the young person' a priority in their vision of the future of British citizenship and of the multicultural nation (2004a and b): 'Engaging with young people is key', reads one Home Office consultation document, 'ensuring that we sow the seeds now of community cohesion in the future ... ensuring that all young people have positive experiences of different cultures and faiths as part of the normal experience of growing up in modern Britain' (Home Office 2004a: 17). The young person of today figures as the multicultural citizen of tomorrow, whose development is constitutive of particular ideas about 'mixing' that found local or national capacity-building strategies aimed at increased integration and cohesion.

This is the political context in which the images examined in this chapter circulated. It is indicative of the ways in which the 'young person' figures as a dense site of investment – political, economic,[4] social, cultural, psychic – in debates about the transmitability, reproduction, and value of the national culture and of the national bond (Berlant 1997; Butler 2002). This context is part of the wider social and cultural moment in which the images discussed here circulated. Though the chapter does not examine politics and strategies of governance *per se*, Kepel's remark about how 'British society was *more* deeply traumatised' (emphasis added) *because* those involved in the attacks in London were 'children of Britain's own multicultural society' points to the depth of purchase that conceptions of the nation/al founded on kinship and bloodlines bring forth. Conceptions in which persons are conceived as property – as 'our' own – and which are inseparable from the national, cultural, and 'racial interests by which these [blood] lines are sustained' (Butler 2002: 15).

My considerations centre on the evocation of the youth figure as it relates to wider anxieties, concerns, desires, and imaginings that haunt the project of national introspection and self-transformation. In what follows, I examine how representations of appealing and unappealing multicultural youth are taken up in the national press, and I discuss their symbolic role and effect on the fantasy structures – the 'sense of reality' – that support and give substance to the national home and the national self; and that keep them whole. The main objective of this chapter is to attend to different figurations of multicultural youth as the lens through which the limits of the imaginative project of Britain are drawn. A characteristic feature of the images here is that they figure multicultural youths that are both like 'us' and not. Insofar as 'mixing' is the privileged trope of accomplished diversity in contemporary Britain, what kinds of 'mixing' are imagined here? How are 'difference' and 'sameness' marked? What kinds of Britain(s), and Britons, are imagined in these figurations? How do they relate to national hegemony and its hierarchies of race, class, gender, and sexuality?

This is about multicultural youth as a 'modal citizen' (Berlant 1997: 21), whose *form* is taken up repeatedly as the reflection, expression, or promise (utopian or dystopian) of the changing nation. The focus on form is paramount to the argument here, given my collection of photographic stills. The figurations discussed here depend upon the very material of the photographic still,[5] and they take place in the relationship between the film membrane and that which lies behind it, which the pellicle conceals or cannot capture. A photograph suggests stillness; it captures a moment but it also suggests timelessness in the sense of being out of time. In this regard, it stabilizes. However, as I show below, a photograph can also bring a depth of disturbance – Barthes (1980) would call this its *punctum* – that questions what we see, and invites us to look for something different *within* the photograph, behind the scene. The stills are the matter of the 'figures' they don't merely represent, but whose existence they (seemingly) evidence; but it is an existence that needs 'filling'. In what follows, I consider the images and, where relevant, their accompanying narratives, the latter constituting ways to fill the photograph with a story, with a past or future, in attempts to make sense of who these 'persons' are, were, or might be.

The chapter includes two sections: 'Models of modern Britons'[6] and 'Monsters of modern Britain'. At one level, this structure follows a 'before and after' 7 July 2005 trajectory to signal the profound turbulence in the national psyche that the attacks in London produced. This is not to suggest that 7/7 was the beginning of new times for Britain that justifies an erasure of the past as no longer relevant (just like 9/11 was said to have changed the world). Still, the summer of 2005 remains a defining moment that forced the recognition that the familiar and the strange shadow each other in uncanny ways. Moving from one section to the other takes us from the 'average Briton' (as the Face of Britain was described) to 'ordinary' Britons (as the suicide-bombers were described) – a delicate shift that is laden with anxieties and broken dreams about the promises of the assimilationist project. How are these figures taken up as embodiments of the possibility of assimilation into, and destabilization of, Britain and Britishness (Lewis 2005: 536)? In the first section, I dissect the images to unravel '[w]hich cultures, or *elements* of cultures, would be "legitimately" included in [this] multiculturalist vision and which would not' (Anthias and Yuval-Davis 1992: 37; emphasis added). Where and what are the limits of legitimate inclusion? The second section considers what happens to the national fantasy frame when the 'other' evades the visibility of cultural difference and becomes uncannily familiar.

Models of modern Britons

The Face of Britain – hereafter also referred to as FoB[7] – was released in most national dailies at the end of March 2001, in the context of intense public debate over the present and future of Britain, the focus of which had moved away from the Parekh Report discussed in the previous chapter and onto the electoral campaign for a new British government. Earlier in the month, the then Conservative Party leader William Hague delivered his infamous 'foreign land' speech, in which he warned against the future of Britain if another Labour government were to be re-elected in the following May's national elections. The speech heavily stressed the dangers of 'open-door' policies regarding asylum-seekers, further entrenching the fear that Britain would be swamped by 'bogus asylum seekers' and that the British people would no longer feel at home in their own land. Later in the same month, media attention was on a row within the Conservative party over the definition of Britishness. The day before Dorley-Brown's image appeared in national newspapers, Conservative MP John Townend declared that 'our homogeneous Anglo-Saxon society has been seriously undermined by the massive immigration – particularly Commonwealth immigration – that has taken place since the [Second World] war' (Sparrow 2001). Though William Hague and numerous other politicians from all parties promptly admonished Townend, the very debate about the multicultural character of Britain suggested that utopian and dystopian conceptions of Britain as a 'mongrel nation' co-exist. Three weeks later, then Foreign Secretary Robin Cook, declared that chicken tikka massala was the British national dish.[8] So we knew what the Face of Britain eats.

It was in this context of clashes between catastrophic and epicurean visions of race relations in Britain that the image was released and celebrated as a portrait of national identity and unity. The photograph was newsworthy in part because of the technological process behind its making, known as 'morphing'. Though it is a technology not new to photography,[9] 'morphing' in contemporary popular culture has become a catchphrase denoting a state-of-the-art graphic special effect that presents images of the mutability of the visible body. Most often associated with computer graphics used in film, video, and television, the 'morph' is the moving image of transformation, through which an object or body appears to reshape itself gradually into another object or body, in full view of the audience.[10] Although the processes of transformation are invisible in static images such as photographs, reporters of Dorley-Brown's image were nonetheless impressed by the result of what they *knew* as the transformation and melding of 1,900 faces into one.[11]

Morphing technology can be used in an array of different ways, including composites that reveal the stitches, collages, juxtapositions, and other traits that actually produce more disturbing images than the Face of Britain. In this respect, the neatness of Dorley-Brown's work stands in stark contrast to, for example, the work of *Mongrel*, an international collective of artists who use digital technologies to create socially engaged and critical cultural productions. One of their projects was 'Colour Separation',[12] which consists of a series of composite skin-masks, each of which appears in various hues. A grey headdress, a pair of eyes that come in different shapes, and a mouth, appear as literally stitched to the skin-mask. The mask seemingly fills a hole in the headdress which is stitched to the skin-mask all around its outer edge. As the artists explain on their website:

> Colour Separation is constructed from photos of over one hundred people who are related in some day-to-day way with the core Mongrel group ... These images wear the masks of the other stereotypes. The masks are spat on. On the cover we have a white man wearing a black mask covered in spit. We have no idea who has done the spitting. Is it a white man fed up of his friend pretending to be black? Has he been spat on because he is a black-masked man who is white underneath?
> (<http://www.mongrel.org.uk/?q = colourseparation> [last accessed 12.02.07])

All the photographs in the project are spat on, and neither the abuser nor the abused are known. Are they spat on for trying to 'pass'? Are they spat on for reducing 'race' to nothing more than fictional stereotypes? One of Mongrel's aims here is to 'reluctantly ... depict the invisible in order to make it disappear', that is, to represent characters that never existed, the 'demonic phantoms of other "races"' that are routinely perceived in society.[13] The insistence on stereotypes forces a reading that goes beyond 'visibility' in the strict sense of what is immediately available to the eye, such as skin colour. 'Colour Separation' is about race as Kalpana Seshadri-Crooks defines it:

Race is fundamentally a regime of looking although race cannot be
reduced to the look. By visibility, I do not mean the deployment of
stereotype whereby all African Americans have dark skin, and all
Caucasians are blond and blue-eyed ... by visibility I refer to a regime
of looking that thrives on 'major' and 'minor' details in order.to shore
up one's symbolic position. It is this concentration on minute difference, perfected by anti-Semitism into a mode of looking, that informs
my model of visibility ... [R]ace [is] a practice of visibility rather than
[a] scientific, anthropological or cultural theory.'

(Seshadri-Crooks 2000: 2)

When looking at the poster with its two-dozen 'masks', all appear at once
alike and different – the 'difference', we are told, being the perceived racial
stereotype. We are asked to 'look' at racial stereotypes, to read the faces
through the lens of race, to find the 'minute differences' even when they are
absent, or when they seem redundant (such as in Yellow Mask/Yellow
Female; Brown Mask/Brown Male; and so on). In short, we are asked to
'do' race as *nothing but* a practice of looking. Whether the invisible ghosts
of 'races' will disappear after they have been revealed in this way, I do not
know. But these portraits make visible the racial ghosts that haunt and
pervade 'the world of common reality' (Gordon 1997: 53) of the present
British political context.

I discuss Mongrel's work at some length to refute the naturalizing tendencies in discourses about morphing technologies as necessarily producing
the 'perfect' image – as if the potential of these technologies somehow
escape the artist or technician who has no power over how individual features will blend into each other. Dorley-Brown's polished image is a far cry
from Mongrel's 'Colour Separation', if only as it conceals, rather than
reveals, the phantoms that the Mongrel collective makes apparent.[14]
Rather, Dorley-Brown's image looks like the photograph of a real person
when in fact it is a cyborg, a human-technology hybrid composed from an
array of photographs of 'real' people. In addition, FoB's 'origins' remain
shrouded in mystery as we cannot access the 'original' photos on the
Haverhill 2000 website where it features (see note 11). Instead, the genealogy begins with the 'first generation' of morphs resulting from the
melding of two photographs. FoB fascinated because s/he is the product of
the magic of morphing technology, which takes stills and de-stills them
into something greater still[15] – the Face of Britain. Concealing the 'real'
faces of Haverhill, concealing the stitches of the technological surgery
involved in melding 1,900 faces, hiding the scars or deformities, concealing
the wrinkles that constitutes the 'individuality of the people who took part
in the project',[16] this morph takes something that's moving (lives, bodies,
the merging of photographs) and makes it still to produce this smoothed-
out youthful face. The Face of Britain was admired for its 'beautifully
proportioned features' (Anonymous 2001; also Bale 2001), which, for its

creator, are a testimony to his 'belief in the attractiveness of the human race' (cited in most newspapers).

Given its alleged mix of people from different ethnic groups, Dorley-Brown's morphing could be seen as refuting cultural and racial roots and essences and as seeking to establish connections between human subjects outside of a racial economy of reproduction. On the website that traces the image's genealogy, the images are organized according to gender and age group, rather than into various racial categories. In this respect, Dorley-Brown's genealogy resists any form of phenotypic indexation: Dorley-Brown does not engage in disaggregating, categorizing, or managing the circulation of the contemporary 'ethnic' or 'racial' subject. On the contrary, the impetus, it seems, is not so much to defend the integrity of cultural difference, but, rather, to preserve the sanctity of the universal.

This universal is deeply wedded to the power of an unmarked whiteness. 'Although the project was designed to produce a virtual representation of Haverhill's population', wrote Stuart Millar in the *Guardian* (2001), 'the photographic artist believes it captures the entire country just as well.' The article continues, quoting the photographer: 'No doubt I would have got different results if I had done it somewhere like Botswana or Mexico.' What would have been the difference? Why would it have been different? The choice of examples is telling: why not France or Canada? And what about other areas of the UK? What if the project had been in London, or Manchester, or Bradford? What if the gender or age distribution of the original subjects had been different? The unsaid assumption is that the face would have been darker (and maybe older?), hence *not* 'capturing' Britain. The whiteness of the face of Britain renders it recognisably British, which I shall return to below. The point I want to make at this stage is that the unarticulated assumptions have a powerful effect: they reinstate and celebrate an assimilationist politics cloaked in universalist claims. Writing in the *Observer* during the row over the Parekh Report in October 2000 (see Chapter 2), the then Home Secretary Jack Straw declared 'we encompass more than one nation and an enormous range of races, accents and attitudes . . . Melding all this into a shared identity was always going to be a challenge' (Straw 2000). The applauded inclusiveness of Dorley-Brown's 'quest to find the average British face' (Bale 2001) is the technological answer to Straw's challenge of melding. This face 'ensures the difference of no difference in the human family' (Haraway 1997: 265). The violence here does not consist in founding the image within a hierarchy of difference based on ideas of racial difference. The violence 'consists instead in the evacuation of histories of domination and resistance... accomplished through morphing as a specific kind of technological (and heterosexual) reproduction' (Castañeda 2002: 96). By denying differences that matter, technology becomes the resolution to histories of domination based on established notions of visible difference.

Claudia Casteñeda argues that '[t]he mutability of the child figured as body in process makes it eminently appropriable [for collective concerns]; not yet fully formed, it has no prior being that must be displaced and then re-placed. It only has to become, according to taste' (2002: 108). With its childlike innocence, the Face of Britain represents the safe, reassuring side of racial mixing. S/he constitutes an appropriate fantasy of a nation that maintains its innocence through the erasure of memory. Decidedly located in the present, this is a body without history: FoB is a youthful face 'with not a line or a wrinkle' (Anonymous 2001), with wrinkles, scars, and other blemishes ironed out, and the marks of personal lives erased, thus being offered up as a blank surface with no past and with only an imagined future rooted in a multicultural present. FoB is a 'national fantasy from the present representing a posthistorical ... future' (Berlant 1997: 201). This photograph projects an image which could represent an actual, existing, human being who could come from *anywhere* in the UK. The portrait of the *'average* 21st century Briton' (S. Millar 2001; emphasis added) is at once unlocated – in history and geography – and aligned to the wider national community, thus becoming the fantasy image of 'the way *we* are' (S. Millar 2001; emphasis added). The Face of Britain also draws its power as a projection of who 'we' are onto a figure 'out there', with a life of its own – the *Daily Mail* (Anonymous 2001) speculated that this could be a young actress, a model, or a member of a boy band – which at the same time is cut off from the social and material relations that define its existence.

Like FoB, similarly youthful and 'beautifully proportioned' are the faces 'Celebrating Multicultural Britain' for the NatWest EMMA Awards 2003 and 2004. The poster from the Ethnic Multicultural Media Academy (EMMA) was launched as emblematic of EMMA's commitment to 'promote multiculturalism'.[17] The three faces in the EMMA poster stand side by side under the heading 'Celebrating Multicultural Britain'. From left to right, the EMMA youths are: a black man, whose face is turned away so that we only see the back of his head and his short hair shaved in the shape of the Union Jack; next to him is a brown-skinned young woman marked as Muslim as she is wearing the Union flag as a head scarf loosely covering her head and shoulders; then, on the left of her, is a young white green-eyed man wearing a trendy hat knitted in the colours and crosses of the Union Jack. In contrast to black EMMA, Muslim and white EMMAs directly face the camera with an expressionless look that stares straight at the onlooker.

A close scrutiny of these faces reveals how the assumed generalized version of successful mixing of which FoB is the fantasy, is grounded in normative processes against which hierarchies of race, class, gender, and sexuality are reinforced. In this sense, being 'white-enough' is not reducible to skin colour. In the present political context whereby to be British is to be moderate, being 'White' is a fantasy frame through which classed, gendered, and sexually-inflected ideas of good citizenship are imagined. The young white man in the EMMA poster, for instance, is telling in this respect. It is worth noting what he is *not* wearing: for example, the hooded sweatshirt, or 'hoodie', which has become the hallmark of white-trash youth known as 'chavs'.[18] Nor is the Union Jack painted on his face or chest in a patriotic gesture associated with the 'ugly face' of extremism and football hooliganism, as mentioned in the previous chapter. His trendy patriotism makes him 'white enough' by being not *too* white, that is, not being too working class (Haylett 2001; Skeggs 2004). Furthermore, he is 'white enough' by not wearing 'non-British' cultural markers: dreadlocks, a turban, a kippa (Jewish skull cap), a kufie (Muslim prayer hat). Hence the white youth here is not 'mixed' as his companions are – he is only part of multicultural Britain by virtue of standing next to 'others'. The integrity of 'white' Britain is preserved and so is the symbolic power of Whiteness as the master signifier, by casting it alongside 'other' visibly hybrid youths.

The focal point of the photograph is the young woman at the centre of the image. Muslim EMMA stands in for 'faith communities' with the Union flag doubling as an Islamic headscarf. The conflation of 'these two overdetermined symbols' (Ahmad 2002: 110) is layered with competing significance. Muneer Ahmad writes about how Arabs, Muslims, and South Asians in the US, after the attacks of September 2001, 'seized the American flag as their own, waving it more fervently, and indeed pre-emptively, embracing the flag as a shield' (2002: 110). This, in his view, constitutes a 'forced reveiling of the community' (2002: 10), in a kind of swap of the veil for the flag. While there are certainly some elements of this also happening in post-9/11 and post-7/7 Britain, there is also a different move operating in the figure of Muslim EMMA. Here the flag and the veil are conflated in a reveiling of the young woman as decidedly British, which is simultaneously a veiling of Britain. This is a very partial, 'loose' veiling – one that is at the moderate end of the continuum of Muslim orthodoxy signalled in women's dress: indeed, this is no burkha,[19] no niqab,[20] or no jilbab,[21] and the headscarf is loosely wrapped around the face, revealing some hair and parts of the neckline, in an aesthetic disciplining of the young South Asian hybrid woman into a 'British enough' Muslim. In addition, and to state the obvious, it is no accident that marks of 'tradition' are specifically drawn on the South Asian woman's body. The mixing of the 'traditional' and the 'modern' are very often figured on South or East Asian women's bodies in representations of global or national multiculturalisms (e.g. Stacey 2000). As agents of integration, Asian women are identified as the preferred subjects moving between cultural borders, while preserving traditions and values. At the same time, we are taught that the Muslim veil, in whatever incarnation, is associated with Islam that in turn is constituted as inherently patriarchal and heterosexist, a point I return to in the following chapter.

Finally, black EMMA, with his hair stylized as the Union Jack, references contemporary trends in black youth culture which are simultaneously marked as ultimately British. A tension arises between a claim to difference and the denial of difference through the flagging of black hair – a politically loaded gesture when we consider the long history of the politics of hair in African American and Black British struggles. Like his Muslim peer, his 'culture' is turned into a national feature. In the rest of my collection of young people's faces, none of the black faces portrayed bear a black cultural marker: no bubu, no dreadlocks, no afro, no stylized haircut. The Union Jack haircut constitutes an aesthetic disciplining of the Black subject into a *British* Black citizen. He is not even looking at the camera, anonymized and kept at distance from the audience looking in, as well as from his peers in the photograph.

Black EMMA, then, is not so much 'white enough', but rather *no longer only* black. In the case of FoB and another young 'face of Britain', Genevieve, their 'blackness' is faded through the gradation of skin colour. Genevieve Capovilla was the subject of an article by Tamsin Blanchard in a special pull-out on 'Race in Britain' published in the *Observer* in November 2001 (Blanchard 2001). Under the title 'Model of a modern Briton', Genevieve is photographed sitting on a low, brick wall, looking enigmatically sideways, her long, thick, and seemingly straightened hair covering her shoulders. She appears pensive and uncertain, neither sad nor happy. For Blanchard, Genevieve, whose mother is Italian and father, West Indian:

> [h]as the enviable quality of looking as though she would be at home *anywhere in the world*. [like the Face of Britain, she is unlocatable] And her look is one that will become increasingly familiar, and – in the worlds of fashion and beauty – increasingly sought after. ... Genevieve is the new English rose. ... At the turn of the twenty-first century ... England's rose has become more of a bronzed, burnished sunflower, equally at home in the Arabian Gulf, the Caribbean or the South China Sea. She is a hybrid, as likely to be part-Indian, Jamaican, Greek, Ethiopian, Japanese or Chinese as the old-fashioned blend of English and Irish.
>
> (Blanchard 2001: 10; emphasis added)

Genevieve's skin is not so much peeled, as seen in Chapter 2, as it is lightened to allow her the mobility that those with unmarked or less marked bodies enjoy, while she is still visibly, and sublimely, 'mixed'. Skin colour, here, becomes a key marker of 'distinction' (Bourdieu 1984). 'Increasingly sought after', the 'bronzed' skin acquires an exchange-value that could provide desirable social and economic capital. Interestingly, the words used to describe Genevieve's skin – 'bronzed, burnished' – are those usually associated with tanned skin, which is coded differently than black skin. The tanned body is a desirable body, a beautiful body, one which signals the care of the self, in contrast to the black, 'stained' body (Ahmed 1998).[22] Similarly, the face of Britain was described as 'youthful, attractive, *olive-skinned*, dark-eyed' (S. Millar 2001; emphasis added). Olive skin, situated between the white and black, is the skin that passes; the one that can be 'at home' anywhere.[23] The appeal of FoB and of Genevieve, it seems, is their skin, more specifically their skin's dual unlocatedness and globality: by being from *any*where, they could go *every*where. These models of modern Britain/Britons offer the promise of a 'new' future for the nation within the globalizing world. 'Enter Genevieve', concludes Blanchard, 'the new girl next door. *The world is yours.*' (2001: 10; emphasis added).

The figure of the multicultural youth, and by extension of the nation, as a mutably racialized body is generated in these figurations of racial and national harmony. Whether in the Face of Britain, Genevieve, or in the EMMA youths enigmatically 'Celebrating Multicultural Britain', multicultural youth is figured through the incorporation of cultural differences and, to paraphrase Castañeda, 'embodies "harmonious" [multicultural] relatedness' (2002: 106). But the message here is that this is a 'harmonious multicultural relatedness' that living in *this* national space makes possible. The models of modern Britons are the nation's fantasized double whose function is to preserve the nation against extinction, reflecting the nation's inherent qualities of tolerance and the timeless tradition of mixing that ensure its strength and immortality by promising a new future. In the models of modern Britons, the nation appears as likeable to itself, as 'what it would like to be', at least for advocates of multiculturalism.[24] This model Briton becomes the nation – as in it 'stands in for' and 'suits' the nation – because it promises to reach beyond the national borders and to establish Britishness as a global, rather than merely local, power. In addition, the model Briton becomes the nation – as in 'it grows up to be' – insofar as it testifies to the national fantasy about its natural capacity to harmoniously incorporate and tolerate differences (cf. Robin Cook's remark in note 8), and to allow hybridized identities and cultures to flourish.

Susan Sontag writes of the surreal effects that result from 'the distance imposed, and bridged, by the photograph: the social distance and the distance in time' (1977: 58). The crafted photographs of FoB, Genevieve, and the EMMA youths have a surreal effect resulting from the distanced, distancing, and enigmatic look of these faces. Their inscrutable, equivocal expression is a substitution for, and a concealment of, the social relations that shape their very formation and circulation *as* embodiments of contemporary multicultural Britain. In addition, it is worth noting that although each of the three EMMAs embodies an individualized version of mixing, they are not mixing among themselves, not engaging with each other. Indeed, they do not appear to be in a very celebratory mood. Utterly individualized and separate, the Muslim and white EMMAs passively stare at the camera, inviting the onlooker to embrace them (or not) in the fantasy narrative of 'Celebrating Multicultural Britain'. This is a celebration of the aesthetic melding of visible difference, a chic notion of hybridity premised upon a reassuring idea of cross-cultural encounter that hides the power relations constitutive of the very conditions surrounding the presence and life of different ethnic groups. That is, the feeling states that these figures appeal to – innocence, quietness, comfort in and promise of the nation/al – are not the kinds of felt embodiments (painful, ambivalent, pleasurable) or the kinds of non-standard identifications (multilocal, multidirectional, multidimensional) experienced by numbers of minoritized 'mixed race' or 'hybrid' children and youth (Ali 2003; Bedell 2003; Frosh *et al.*, 2002; Gorham 2003; Kennedy-McFoy 2006; Lewis 2004a; Tizard and Phoenix 2002). The striking thing about these figures is that their very form – the expressionless face – constitutes an exemplary anonymity and quietness that mirrors the formlessness – the generic significance, unlocatedness, a-historicality, undecidability – of the universal, abstract, 'average' subject-citizen (Berlant 2001: 46). This 'average' citizen inhabits the fantasy world of New Labour's Britain, where 'mixing', like 'melding' and 'morphing', becomes a sanitized version of miscegenation that not only evacuates histories of domination and resistance, but that re-establishes Britishness-as-Whiteness, while it simultaneously fetishizes the colour of the 'ethnic' as desirable if 'white enough'. The particular 'ethnic other' stands in for the generalized nation thus disavowing Whiteness as a regime of looking, as 'a system of ordering the world, a discourse of differences' (Seshadri-Crooks 2000: 97) that imperceptibly maintains the '*other*' as the exception. The appeal of the models of modern Britons is not that they all *look* white – they don't – but that they *act* 'White' (see King 2004; Gilroy 2001) – their expressionless faces suggest a discreet quietness that has nothing of the excesses of young rioters and angry Muslims whose actions confirm their alienness from Britishness. As Lauren Berlant might put it, this is 'a future race of cyborgs, or mixed-race but still white-enough children' (Berlant 1997: 207). In addition, the Union flag and other means of 'flagging the nation' (Billig 1995) – such as the headlines and articles describing FoB – re-roots and re-routes the multicultural as *truly British*. This fantasy of multicultural Britain nurtures the 'national vanity' (Berlant, 1997: 196) and is part of a recurring motif identified in the previous chapter: that of rewriting the national same so that 'we' could love ourselves as different.

Genevieve is an apposite embodiment of this new national self. In the *Observer* article (Blanchard 2001), Genevieve is saluted as 'the New English rose', as the model for the 'controversial new "mixed" category of the 2001 census [that] attracted 400,000 ticks'. As such, she is hailed as the promise of and figure for 21st-century multiracial Britain. Now being held as an identity in Britain – a 'race of its own' as Tamsin Blanchard puts it (2001; see also Parker and Song 2001b: 7) – 'mixed' is at risk of being further naturalized in terms that suggest that the problems or advantages that individuals encounter 'are somehow intrinsic to the group rather than dependent on social processes' (Olumide in Ali 2003: 4). Jill Olumide argues that the institutionalization of 'mixed race' naturalizes it as a viable social category. The naturalization of 'mixed race' is in part a result of the ways in which nation, cultural background, and race are conflated in the very construction of the 'mixed' identity – as in 'White British', or 'Black Caribbean' – which leads to the racialization of national–cultural groupings. In addition, conceptions of racial intermixing privilege the black/white binary framework, thus excluding a plethora of other potential identifications and forms of mixedness (Ali 2003: 5), while privileging whiteness as a necessary part of the mix.[25] But another element usually overlooked by critics of 'mixed race' is the naturalization of heterosexual, reproductive love, which is part and parcel of accepted conceptions of mixed race. Indeed, the 'mixed race' child is always already assumed to be the offspring of heterosexual marriage. If the models of modern Britons such as Genevieve or Haverhill's morph are hailed because they are seen as transcending racial economies of difference, there remains, however, a *necessary* connection that operates through heterosexuality. Hybridity is a resolutely heterosexual category (Young 1995: 26; also Dyer 1997).

Heterosexual love is a key site where both the limits and potential of multiculturality are embattled. On the one hand, the far-right British National Party's (BNP) appeal to ethnic minorities as potential allies in the July 2001 issue of their magazine *Identity*, clearly framed the new relationship as 'Friends *not* family, cooperation *not* membership' (in Back 2001; emphasis BNP's). The shift away from the BNP's earlier antagonistic approaches to inter-ethnic relations is contained within an anti-miscegenation discourse in which the limits of acceptable 'mixing' are drawn along bodily lines of heterosexual reproduction. As a senior member of the BNP and councillor for Barking and Dagenham (North East London), Richard Barnbrook, recently stated, 'I'm not opposed to mixed marriages but their children are washing out the identity of this country's indigenous people' (in Taylor 2007).[26]

In opposition to this stance, centre-left thinkers invoke marriage as the ultimate symbol of achieved multiculturalism. In October 2000, Lady Gavron, vice-chair of the Commission on the Future of Multi-Ethnic Britain, reportedly declared: 'It would have been great if Prince Charles had been told to marry someone black. Imagine what message that would have sent out' (in Thomson 2000). 'A mixed-race royal wedding', she said, 'would have sent out the right message about racial integration' (in Doughty 2000c). Yasmin Alibhai-Brown, for her part, states that 'Every mixed-race marriage is building a better Britain' (in Parker and Song 2001b: 19n18).[27] Heterosexual interracial love and marriage are regarded as emblems of both the threatening and emancipating pathways towards the achievement of a fully multicultural nation.

Certainly, the defence of mixed-race unions is an anti-racist rebuke to BNP's (and other far right organisations) order not to mix in the name of racial purity. Still, the insistence on marriage as the preferred mode of mixing bolsters the nationalist ideology of the family as the cornerstone of society.

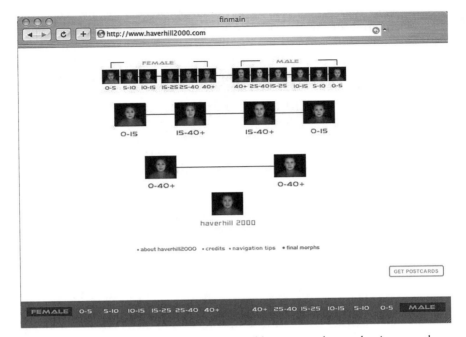

Figure 3.2 Face of Britain's genealogy. Virtual heterosexual reproductive acts; the 'final morphs' leading to the generation of Haverhill's 'Face of Britain'. Courtesy of Chris Dorley-Brown and Haverhill Town Council.

It returns us to a model of human bonding through heterosexual kinship, 'the family', and recognizable intimate relations as they are organized and legitimated in the institution of marriage. In this regard, claims in support of, as well as against, interracial marriage and heterosexual reproduction are similarly complicit in restricting the domain of what is recognizable as 'legitimate sexual arrangements', 'while in no way disrupting the patrilineal assumptions of kinship or the project of the unified nation that it supports' (Butler 2002: 26, 16). Consider the genealogy of Haverhill's Face of Britain presented on the Haverhill 2000 website (Figure 3.2). While the alleged ethnic origins of the Face of Britain are unmarked, the sexual differentiation is clearly demarcated. Visitors to the website can navigate between the different 'generations' [sic] of morphings, leading to the 'final morphs' which are organized in a recognizable genealogical arborescent structure. Moving from top to bottom, males and females are gradually coupled to produce the 'parents' of the final morph. The genealogy of the morph reveals that it has been bred through virtual heterosexual reproductive acts.

If mixed-race youth are destabilizing because they suggest a mutably racial national body and reveal the instability of *visible* bodily differences, they are also reassuring because their very existence alleviates anxieties about the fluidity and *invisibility* of sexual difference. The issue of interracial love is often conflated with that of interracial kinship, where 'the child figures in the debate as a dense site for the transfer and reproduction of culture' (Butler 2002: 22) and of national unity and hegemony, both of which are laced with norms of racial purity and domination. To put it simply, the potential anxieties over the uncanniness of the new Face of Britain – FoB's 'spooky gender free' ambiguity (S. Millar 2001) as well as his/her racial queerness – are deflected through his/her genealogy steeped in heterosexuality, and in the reassertion of hetero-normativity as a condition of social membership. Hence the bond to the nation gets figured as the prerogative of heterosexuality, and the product of this bond, the *legitimate offspring* of this bond, is the promise of the future.

If models of modern Britons are white enough, they are also to be moderately and successfully heterosexual. Muslim EMMA's veil remains marked as belonging to what is widely conceived of as an inherently patriarchal and heterosexist culture, whose familial arrangements do not fit in the fantasy structure of the heterosexual home of the nation (more in the next chapters). The young models of modern Britons can slide into treason and perversion if they come from the 'wrong' family. As Paul Gilroy (2002) has pointed out, alongside the celebration of cool Britannia's mixed-race celebrity children[28] – Zadie Smith, Kelly Holmes, Daley Thompson, Scary Spice, Sade – came the announcement of the failures of multiculturalism confirmed by the likes of 'shoe bomber' Richard Reid, whose pathologized family history initially served to obscure the conditions that produce social disaffection, and to disown him from any claims to Britishness. Following his arrest in December 2001 for attempting to blow up American Airlines Flight 63 from Paris to Miami by igniting explosives hidden in the soles of his shoes,[29] stories circulated in the press and television about his mixed-race background and his upbringing in an all white family – his mother Leslie Hughes remarried a white British man after divorcing his black Jamaican father Robin Reid. As the *Guardian* reported, the 'mixed race kid in a white family … was the genesis of his problems. He was trying "to sort out where he was from, his roots. He wanted to find out an identity – but he's got two white parents"' (Nzerem 2002). Richard Reid was 'proof' of the failures of multiculturalism, not because of the mixing as such, but because it was the wrong mix: the relationship between his 'ill-matched' parents from different class backgrounds – he a railway worker of Jamaican extraction who turned to petty crime, she the daughter of an accountant and magistrate from the north-east – 'seems to have put an early strain on their marriage' (Seaton 2002).

Reid's damaged sense of self was widely conceived as originating from his troubled family history: his 'mixed race' and cross-class but *failed* heterosexual parentage. The containment of his acts within his own psyche simultaneously quarantines him as a monstrous human being and identifies the perverse familial conditions that lead to pathology. Reid disfigures the fantasy model of modern Britons: the canny beauty of multicultural Britain becomes uncannily 'other' in Reid's story. And in the aftermath of the arrests of suspected terrorist plotters in August 2006, Reid's photograph resurfaced as part of a wider cast of 'home-grown' terrorists – these 'children of multicultural Britain' who now haunt the scenario of successful multicultural integration. Again, much effort was put into attempts to quarantine the young bombers in pathologized psyches. But in contrast to narratives about Reid in 2002, the pathology was now attributed to a whole religious cultural forma-tion that was allowed to thrive, according to some sections of the press, because of the naïve benevolence of multiculturalist politics. As I argue below, the figurations of the terrorist 'children of multicultural Britain' highlight the ambivalence of Britain as fantasy home.

Monsters of modern Britain

The news photographs this week are of ordinary English two- and three-bedroom houses in Micklefield Road and Hepplewhite Close, in Belchers Lane and Plomer Green Avenue – ordinary English roads with the sorts of names that usually we find comforting.

(Robson 2006)

Even for outsiders, family photographs often have a poignant quality, perhaps because they speak all too unerringly of the insufficiency, the hopelessness, of the desire they embody. Time has passed, time will pass.

(Kuhn 2002: 50)

The front page of the *Guardian* of 14 July 2005 showed a large 10" x 6" photograph of 20-year old Shahara Islam, killed in the Number 30 bus that was blown up by Hasib Hussain in Tavistock Square seven days earlier. The byline above it read as follows:

She was 20 years old, from Plaistow, east London. He was 18, from Holbeck, Leeds. Both were from close-knit families – one Bengali, the other Pakistani. Both were Muslims. Hasib Hussain became a suicide-bomber. Shahara Islam became his victim.

Under the photograph, two headlines:

The bomber Boy   **The Victim** Modern
who didn't stand out   – and still traditional

The two articles that followed, one on each individual, emphasized how their lives mirrored each other yet took dramatically different paths that would forever bind their fates. Aside from the normatively gendered characterization of Shahara as studious, hardworking, modern *and* traditional – a model of a modern Briton – and of Hasib as a slightly unruly but 'normal' [sic] youth with no particular talent for academic subjects or sports, the whole report was replete with remarks about the 'unremarkable' character of both Hasib and Shahara. Hasib is described as having been a 'normal, unremarkable pupil', an 'unremarkable young man' whose inexplicable transformation that led him to 'turn his back on his life in Holbeck' was deemed a conundrum that was not to be easily resolved (Cobain 2005). Shahara, for her part, was described as a 'thoroughly modern Muslim' young woman who 'loved her Burberry plaid handbag and fashionable clothes', who also respected 'her family's wishes that she sometimes wore traditional shalwar kameez at home' (Gillan 2005). Her public persona was contrasted starkly to her private one – to the point that owners and customers of cafes near her workplace and where she was a regular customer, reportedly failed to recognize the smiling young woman dressed in turquoise silk in the newspaper pictures of missing persons after the bombs. 'I saw her in her mainstream clothing', the owner of Patisserie Bliss is quoted as saying.

> She was eloquent in her speech, a very confident upright sort of girl. She had a nice manicure and her hair was always straightened. She didn't look like some stereotyped ethnic minority.
>
> (Gillan 2005)

The likeness of both Hasib and Shahara – not only were they 'alike' but they were 'like us' and not like 'stereotyped' others – signalled yet another, albeit subtle, shift in the visual referent of the nation/al. From not-quite-white-but-white-enough, the Muslim Briton is here 'unremarkable' but still potentially radically 'other'.

In stark contrast to the images of the model Britons, Shahara's photograph has the hallmarks of a family snapshot rather than the features of the professional, polished, artistic and depersonalized photos of Genevieve, EMMA, or the Face of Britain. Her smiling face looks directly at the camera, and she is posed against a dark background. She is wearing hoop earrings, and her uncovered hair falls loose over her shoulders. A blue silk scarf is wrapped around her neck, maybe part of the 'traditional' silk garb she is said to occasionally adorn out of 'respect' for her parents' wishes. This was a young adult, successful, respectable, and respectful, liked by her workmates and loved by her family. The model daughter, she was also the model hybrid-Briton, who successfully melded the traditional and the modern by keeping them separate, in their place – at least from the point of view of those she interacted with in the workday. She held such promise

Figure 3.3 Shehzad Tanweer. Courtesy of the Ross Parry Agency.

until her life was tragically and brutally brought to an end. The photograph is evidence not only of time that has inexorably passed, but of a life that has tragically and prematurely ended.

Like Shahara, the photographs of the suicide-bombers that circulated in the press following the attacks in July 2005 were remarkable for their ordinariness. With the exception of Hasib Hussain,[30] the bombers all featured in photos of daily, mundane, activities. In one photograph that circulated widely, Mohammad Sidique Khan is shown in a classroom with a colleague, engaged in what appears as a teaching session or a meeting; his face is in a half-smile, attentive to what a female colleague next to him is saying.[31] Another photo, of Germaine Lindsay (Abdullah Shaheed Jamal) and his wife and young child, sitting on a settee, maybe in their home, shows a happy couple smiling at the camera.[32] The child is on the mother's lap, facing the camera; she is holding him with her right arm across his little chest, and her face is nestled between the child's and the father's. The child's face has been technologically blurred to avoid recognition – a gesture that turns the ordinary family photo into a press photograph available for the public to see and study. That blurring – which also covers the face of Khan's colleague – protects the identity of those close to the bombers. The anodyne, banal snapshots have been subjected to professional reprocessing following the legal conventions for protection, while they also circulate as nothing more than banal, anodyne, and utterly recognizable to thousands and millions of outsiders who have similar snaps in their own family collections.

The most striking photograph is Shehzad Tanweer's school photograph (Figure 3.3). Here we have the small school-photograph of a young boy.

We only see his face and a bit of his neckline and shoulders. We see the narrow collar of a white shirt neatly rolled over a black jumper. The boy is smiling shyly at the camera, his short hair tidy – perhaps the boy had combed it or hastily passed his fingers through it just before entering the room where the photo was taken. The photograph is so recognizable it *pierces* me, as Barthes (1980) would put it. It reminds me of one particular school photograph of mine, and if I were to set it next to this one, one might surmise that he and I had been at the same school. This is the school photograph that parents would order in different sizes: some for the wallets, some for the family album, some to set in a frame. From where was this photo extracted? A family album? A frame on the mantelpiece? The hands of a sobbing mother or father clutching at the photo of their child? There is something disturbingly intimate about Tanweer's photo; it is poignant precisely for its familiarity. It is made from the template of 'school photographs' – in which the child figure is a '*tabula rasa*, an empty slate, on which [parents' and teachers'] own desires could be written' (Kuhn 2002: 51).[33] Tanweer's photograph bears the hallmarks of a family-collection photo, with the associated fantasies of happiness and comfort it carries. There is preciousness to the family photograph and to the narrative it is cast into within the family album – a visual narrative that keeps a sense of the family safe, and hence the photograph is kept safe under a clear plastic sheet in a bound album. But now wrenched from its place of safe keeping, this photograph has become public property, circulating, like Shahara's image, as evidence of a moment and a life past, testimony to the ordinary child that he was. It is available for all to see, to study; for all to witness the hopelessness of the desire it embodies, to paraphrase Kuhn from the epigraph to this section; the hopelessness of the fantasy of the boy as the screen of his (national) family's desires.

Although we could create a narrative around photographs, there is nothing in the photographs *themselves* that tells us how to read them – the family photo masks the 'family secrets' (Kuhn 2002), that is the turbulences that disrupt the family harmony. The photograph 'cannot *say* what it lets us see' (Barthes 1981: 100). Often, the family album will be riddled with captions or headings to provide bits of information that are otherwise unavailable. In addition, with the family-album photograph, viewers are invited to read back into the image, to find the adult in the photograph of the child. Similarly with the Face of Britain, readers were invited to read back into the photograph, to look for others *inside* it, to seek out a telltale detail that might divulge the presence of more than what can be seen. If photographs are about bridging time that has passed (Kuhn 2002: 50; Sontag 1977: 48) by reading back into them, there is, however, no reading forward: the photograph itself will not reveal how the child will turn out; or if she or he will be violent. The depths of the photographs of the 7/7 bombers lie beyond them. Family members, neighbours,

Figure 3.4 CCTV *still, Luton Station, London, 7 July 2005.* London bombing suspects (L-R) Hasib Mir Hussain, Germaine Lindsay, Mohammed Sadique Khan and Shehzad Tanweer are seen at Luton train station, north of London, in this 7 July 2005 Closed Circuit Television video footage released by London's Scotland Yard on 16 July 2005. Courtesy of REUTERS/Scotland Yard.

co-workers, co-religionists, and former teachers were interviewed by journalists in an effort to piece together the bombers' life stories that would 'fill' the pictures and compile the stuff of life that the photographs themselves could not reveal. These were also attempts to read back into the photographs, as it were, and to excavate early signs of violence.

The resulting narratives invariably turned up 'ordinary' lives of 'ordinary' men: 'the nice lad' (Hussain), 'the teacher' (Sidique Khan), 'the cricketer' (Tanweer), the 'Jamaican-born father' (Lindsay/Jamal). The narratives about these men's lives also came with press photographs of 'ordinary' streets where these 'ordinary' men resided in 'ordinary' houses. The narratives culminated in the last available image of the four men alive: the grainy still from the CCTV cameras in Luton railway station showing the four men entering the station carrying their lethal rucksacks on that dreadful morning of 7 July 2005 (Figure 3.4). Like the family photographs, the CCTV stills could not capture the activity before and after the arrival of the four young men at the station. Reprinted on the front page of the *Observer* (17 July 2005) (among many other reprints), the caption underneath the image read:

It [the still] is extraordinary for its ordinariness ... There is nothing in the image to suggest the atrocity that was to follow, that the four men carrying rucksacks were the four bombers intent on creating havoc in London later that morning. Dressed casually and appearing relaxed, they could be any group of friends starting a day out.

These narratives of ordinariness gave a different depth to the photographic stills; their wide and reiterated circulation solidified the meanings attached to the photographs, while simultaneously and uncannily multiplying their contexts. The insistence on the ordinariness of the men's lives and appearance made them relocatable anywhere in the ordinary streets and homes from which they were coaxed.[34] Because of their circulation alongside the reconstructed biographies of the four men, these photos are not of one singular person but of a co-presence, of 'what has been' and of 'what will be': the innocent child, ordinary father, teacher, *and* the suicide-bomber. The ghost of the suicide-bomber haunts the figure of the innocent child of multicultural Britain – including Shahara, who is haunted by the ghost of her killer, Hasib Hussain. And as Roland Barthes puts it, we 'observe with horror an anterior future of which death is the stake' (1980: 150; my translation). Because of the events that brought the photos to the public eye in the first place, a depth or 'blind field is created ... is divined' (Barthes 1981: 57) around the photographs figuring 'ordinary' Muslim Britons, especially youths. This is a depth that is no longer of form – like FoB – but of time – 'it's only a question of time'. Once the images are made to allow for that kind of depth of disturbance, *any* image can be read that way. Shahara is not only haunted by her killer, she is also haunting because there is nothing that distinguishes her 'ordinariness' from Hasib's apart from her gender and ethnic origins – one visible, but the other invisible within the White British scopic regime of difference. Indeed, Shahara and Hasib's stories are cast as being alike – Hasib's life is said to have 'in some ways mirrored' [sic] Shahara's – both were Muslim, from South-Asian 'close-knit families', second generation, ordinary young people. Furthermore, Hasib and the other three suicide-bombers of July 2005 were similarly 'ordinary' and their unremarkable lives were difficult to distinguish from their other Muslim neighbours' lives. 'Thus we have characters who are to be considered identical because they look alike' (Freud 1955: 234): unremarkable, religious but ostensibly moderate Muslims.

That which separates the model from the monstrous Britons is a thin film that gradually disappeared as more photographs and biographies of other 'ordinary' British Muslims circulated in the written and televisual press in August 2006, following the arrest of 15 people on suspicion of an alleged plot to blow up flights bound to the US from the UK.[35] The thinning out of the distance between models and monsters was cast in deep connection to the reduction of the distance between 'us' and 'them', as the distance no longer appeared as clearly discernable. Indeed, in August 2006, more photographs of 'ordinary' streets and houses – random photographs it seemed – were repeatedly printed in the national dailies to reiterate the extraordinariness of the ordinariness and anonymity of those who can commit such atrocious acts. The *Independent* front page headline on 12 August 2006 asked 'The enemy within?' with photographs of run-of-the-mill terraced houses and street names (Folkestone Rd, Hepplewhite Close, Walton Drive, Albert Rd) that the *Express*'s David Robson describes as '*usually* ... comforting' (emphasis added) in the epigraph to this section. That added word, 'usually', suggests a new discomfort in what is known as home. Robson, among numerous others in the national press, was forced to face the very uncertainty about home and by extension, about the national self. If, as argued above, the models of modern Britons are the nation's fantasized doubles that mirror the nation's multicultural present and project a promising future, in the photographs of the terrorist youth of multicultural Britain, 'the "double" reverses its aspects. From having been an assurance of immortality, it becomes the uncanny harbinger of death' (Freud 1955: 235), consequently producing a deep national 'ego-disturbance' (Freud 1955: 236). If the uncanny beauty of models of modern Britons such as FoB protect the fantasy of Britain as a tolerant, benevolent, feel-good place to be, the horror of the suicide-bombers deeply perturbs the fantasy frame through which reality can be assessed and brings the violence of the world we live in *at the heart of home,* at the heart of the national self (Salecl 2004: 24; also Žižek 1998). As Priscilla Wald writes, 'the uncanny sends us home to the discovery that "home" is not what or where we think it is and that we, by extension, are not who or what we think we are' (1995: 7).

In (post)colonial Britain, the fantasy frame of national wholeness and distance is constituted through imaginative geographies (Said 1978) that:

> are constructions that fold distance into difference through a series of spatializations. They work ... by multiplying partitions and enclosures that serve to demarcate 'the same' from 'the other', at once constructing and calibrating a gap between the two by 'designating in one's mind a familiar space which is "ours" and an unfamiliar space beyond "ours" which is "theirs".' 'Their' space is often seen as the inverse of 'our' space: a sort of negative, in the photographic sense that 'they' might 'develop' into something like 'us'.
>
> (Gregory 2004: 17)

In present-day Britain, where 'there' is now 'here' in the bodies of migrants, imaginative geographies separate 'us' from 'them' through spatial partitionings such as the private–public divide deployed in Shahara's story. This separation constitutes and maintains difference at a distance, while surrounding her with an aura of beauty – docile, traditional and modern, 'integrated' – that reassures the nation of its benevolence and tolerance for privatized/domesticated difference. Likewise, the insistence on the alleged connections of the bombers with Al Qaeda, Afghanistan, Pakistan, or with foreign-born clerics, and the obstinate refusal of Tony Blair to recognize any link with Britain's war on terror and international politics in Iran, Afghanistan, and Lebanon, repeatedly projects the terrorists' motivations and education outside of *this* national frame.[36] At the same time, the repeated accounts of the ordinary lives of the terrorists dissolved the distance between 'here' and 'there', 'us' and 'them', and the other became uncannily familiar. Britain's 'world of common reality' (Gordon 1997: 53) is now haunted by that which is inseparable from its self. Indeed, for Freud, the uncanny 'derives its terror not from something externally alien or unknown but – on the contrary – from something strangely familiar which *defeats our efforts to separate ourselves from it.'* (Morris 1985; emphasis added) As the distance of the colonial past is merged into the colonial present, so do distances fold into closeness and differences meld into likeness. And that likeness is what is uncannily haunting.

The Face of Britain is precisely about that movement from the negative to the positive in the photographic process of 'them' literally developing *into* something like us – to the point of being indistinguishable. The combined photographic and biographical portraits of the 'enemies within', for their part include stories of how they have 'developed' like us: s/he is educated, a cricket-lover, a fan of *Only Fools and Horses* (Robson 2006), has a taste for fish and chips (Robson 2006) or Highland Shortcakes (Gilroy 2004b), a good quiet husband, father, mother, a 'nice neighbour', speaks English inflected with a regional accent. These individuals were and are utterly integrated not simply in British popular culture and a British 'lifestyle and work', as Tony Blair put it (2006) – 'what, on the face of it, could be more integrated than a love for Only Fools and Horses?' (Robson 2006) – but they are also integrated into a global world of warfare and economic inequality marked and signified in civilizationist, racialized terms.

Here were 'ordinary' men leading 'ordinary lives' who planned extraordinary crimes. Similarly in August 2006, the 'unremarkableness' of the suspected attackers became a mantra-like reiteration of their terrifying invisibility and forced (yet again) the realization of the limits of a regime of looking that combined skin colour with cultural markers – the veil, the beard, the tunic – in order to shore up and secure the investment in Britain's symbolic position as the master white nation. Moreover, 'difference' and 'sameness' are always continually redefined as populations change or individuals appropriate the codes of acceptable appearance. For example, some bombers were said to have shaved their beards and traded their Muslim garb for 'ordinary' clothing. It all came to a head when 27-year-old Brazilian Jean Charles de Menezes was shot dead by Metropolitan Police officers at Stockwell tube station on the morning of 22 July 2005, because, according to the police, his clothing and behaviour were suspicious. The tragic death of de Menezes brought into relief the extent to which the perception of the human body, with its various discursive, material, and institutional technologies of differentiation and categorization, 'has very little to do with anatomy and is in fact all to do with language, fantasies and the unconscious' (Salecl 2004: 46).

The swiftness with which suggestions were put forward for identity cards in 2005 and for profiling in 2006 is indicative of the deep anxieties that the prospect of losing sight of difference could trigger. Freud relates the uncanny to the fear of loosing one's eyes, which he sees as a fear of castration, in which the eyes are a surrogate for the male sexual organ. The 'monsters' of modern Britain rob the 'master Britain' from its omnipotent power to see, to demarcate, then to erase difference in its self-proclaimed capacity to absorb differences into a rich diversity. In forcing the nation to now look at itself from where it is observed – from the 'other within' – rather than to look at and identify with the image in which the nation appears likeable to itself, but still at a distance, the bombers of 7/7 and their suspected brothers were seen as 'more' disturbing because they were *of* Britain. Thus, they struck directly at national self-love because they were seen to try to take it away out of their alleged hate of what Britain is supposed to be all about: the celebration of multiculture (Blair 2006).

The uncanny beauty of 'us'

The images and narratives of 'children of multicultural Britain' that circulated in the British public domain between 2001 and 2006 solidified their meaning as models or monsters *of Britain*. That is, 'multicultural youth' is figured as a national property and, therefore, stands in a testimony to the nation's success or failure in domesticating its 'children'. Thus, whatever the pleasures or fears the images are seen as provoking, they are re-routed and contained within a fantasy frame that supports the belief in the primacy and unifying force of the *nation* (the national 'we'). Consider public commentator Will Hutton's[37] reflections in the *Observer*, in the summer of 2005, which are worth quoting at length.

> Britain, the writ of Britishness and what seems obvious to the rest of us leaves a critical mass of British Muslims cold; they refuse to believe what is palpably true. Whatever mix of responses you think are needed to lift the threat of the bombs ... part of the story will have to be persuading young British Muslims that Britishness is an idea worth a minimal degree of loyalty that inhibits mass murder ... The problem for Pakistanis, Eritreans and Somalians is that the tribe to which they emotionally belong within the British accommodation does not command anything like the same loyalty as being British English, British Indian or even British Jamaican. Being British and English, or British and Indian works; being British Pakistani or Eritrean does not. They come from broken-backed countries that have no proud history, culture or

identity – Pakistan, for example, is only 58 years old: the identity that makes more proud sense is Islam. And in one jump young British Muslim Somalians, Eritreans and Pakistanis are suddenly in the vortex of a culture and religion profoundly wounded by globalisation, Western foreign policy and its own failure to match the rise of Christendom – with all its capacity to transmute a doctrine of peace into a doctrine of sexism, murder and anti-semitism.

(Hutton 2005)[38]

Hutton's comments suggest a failure to think beyond the national frame, and express a strong belief in the promise of a 'strong nation' as the necessary condition for (national) self-love. He invokes the image of the broken-backed, damaged, weak nation that cannot provide a solid enough ground for its subjects.[39] The post-7/7 discussions and suggestions for strengthening pride in Britishness were based on the narcissistic assumption that the suicide-bombers hated the British 'we' and had refused to find any pride in being British. The paradox is that the nation is assumed to be under threat from the Other who wants to steal from the national people their narcissistic enjoyment of their nation and of themselves as nationals, 'even as it is suggested ... that *they* cannot possibly grasp' that enjoyment (Harney 2006: 374; emphasis original). Because the young British Muslims originate from weak nations, according to Hutton, they cannot grasp the pleasure of the symbolic power of the nation, of the 'writ of Britishness'.

Hutton seems to have utter faith in the redemptive powers of what Žižek (1993) calls the 'Nation Thing' which cannot be reducible to a shared way of life. What is 'palpably' true, to Hutton, is an '*idea*', the Thing that:

> binds the national community together through a sense of shared enjoyment even as this element escapes symbolic identification. It suggests something more, an unrepresentable sense of a common bond, a shared, tacit, indescribable knowledge to members of the community... The Nation Thing is a restricted space for the national community to organize its enjoyment, which is premised on the tacit knowledge and sense of pleasure in the surety that the nation provides a stable source of identification, a sense of security, and unity.
>
> (Harney 2006: 374)

For Hutton, would-be suicide-bombers are those who lack a bond with their 'original' national community and who are thus incapable of grasping it in Britain. Yet the insistence on the 'writ' of Britishness and its 'obviousness' conceals the very ambivalence of the nation/al's enjoyment of itself. In Britain's precarious state of post-colonial melancholia (Gilroy 2004a), perceptions of the 'home-grown' terrorists hit particularly hard at the ambivalent pleasure and guilt about the colonial foundations of contemporary

Britain as they lead the nation/al 'back to what is known of old and long familiar' (Freud 1955: 220).

> For this uncanny is in reality nothing new or alien, but something which is familiar and old-established in the mind and which has become alienated from it only through the process of repression ... something which ought to have remained hidden but has come to light.
>
> (Freud 1955: 241)

The deeply unsettling spectre of the home-grown terrorists brings home the repressed ambivalence towards Britain's past and present colonial endeavours and fantasies. As reminders of Britain's colonial past and present, the terrorist 'children of multicultural Britain' unsettle – unlike their 'model' counterparts – because their stories cannot be reconciled with the official national story of past and present achievements in 'developing' others into being 'like us'. They unsettle because they are seen to falsify that story or 'reveal it to be incomplete' (Marks 2000: 51).

The figures discussed in this chapter, and the different histories they conjure up, erase, or promise, dramatically highlight the very ambivalence of the nation's idea or knowledge of itself. Though the images examined may have originated in different times, they co-exist within Britain's multicultural horizons, and together they force the recognition of the very ambivalence of the nation/al as both *heimlich* and *unheimlich*, a thing of beauty and comfort, and a thing of dread and death. It is a thin line that separates the 'model' from the 'monster' and beauty from ugliness. Žižek argues that beauty, like fantasy, acts as a screen – the film, the pellicle – that protects, 'encloses, overcoats, [a thing's] interior, whereas in the case of ugliness, an excess of interiority threatens to overwhelm and engulf the subject' (Žižek 1998: 166). Following on from that, beauty and ugliness could be seen as both sides of the split subject; the split that fantasy is meant to hide. Thus it is not simply that the beautiful faces are fantasies that protect against the ugly faces. The ugly faces are constitutive of the fantasy insofar as, first, they are that which the fantasy protects us against. Second, they are themselves fantasized as utterly other, in an attempt to separate them from the 'average' Briton – in an attempt to further hide the split constitutive of the national. When considered together, the different Britains/Britons that the figurations bring forth reveal the deep ambivalence of Britain's conception of 'the other within' who is expected to display not too much, not too little, but just enough alterity *of the right kind*: moderately religious, successfully heterosexual, not-too-White but White-enough. If, following Freud (1955), we accept that *heimlich* and *unheimlich* are both sides of the same coin, then the multicultural youth could be read as representations of the uncanniness of national domestication.

This chapter excavates the double process of *rapprochement* and distancing, of desiring and containing cultural difference, as it operates differently on different bodies – especially but not exclusively on minoritized bodies. Who is close to whom, to what extent, and what are the limits? What happens when 'they' become so like us that we can no longer tell the difference? The next chapter continues this exploration, but this time centres on white working-class Britons. What happens to the project of domestication when young, white Britons get too close to undesirable 'others' and excessively take them on – in both senses of 'taking on', as in adopting and confronting?

4 Loving thy neighbour and the politics of inter-ethnic propinquity

> It is unfashionable to speak of loving one's neighbour, but unless our society can move at least to a position where we can respect our neighbours as fellow human beings, we shall fail in our attempts to create a harmonious society in which conditions have changed so radically in the last 40 years.
>
> (Home Office 2001a: 20)

In October 2003, a documentary on Channel 4 raised some concern in the British press about the future of white Britain. *Cutting Edge: The Last White Kids*, directed by Shona Thompson (Thompson 2003),[1] is a documentary about the Gallagher family who live in Manningham, an area in Bradford, West Yorkshire (northern England), and who are 'the only white family' remaining in a street with a predominance of Muslim residents (predominantly of Pakistani and Bangladeshi background). With its title clearly echoing Enoch Powell's 'Rivers of Blood Speech',[2] the film suggests from the outset that white Britain is disappearing in the face of the threats posed by invasive multiculture.

Filmed during the summer of 2003, the documentary opens with a shot of schoolchildren spilling out of a school playground, the majority of whom are girls wearing headscarves. After a few silent minutes, the voice-over informs us that 'this is a story about white children growing up in a world where nearly everyone else is a different colour from them.' This comment sutures the meaning of the image on the screen where headscarves, not skin colour, are the dominating feature. By conflating colour with faith, the film immediately marks religion as a racial issue. The headscarf is the new black.

It is in this frame that we are introduced to Sharon Gallagher and her three children and invited to consider how 'such intense exposure to a different culture has affected each child differently', as one *Guardian* commentator put it (Manzoor 2003). Sharon Gallagher's two daughters, Amie, aged 9, and Ashlene, aged 12, are drawn to Islam – 'intoxicated' according to another *Guardian* reviewer (McLean 2003). They attend the local mosque, wear headscarves, and wish to convert to Islam. Their 8-year-old cousin Lauren also occasionally wears headscarves to school. In stark contrast, the girls' brother, Jake Gallagher, 11, and their cousins John, 9, and Devlin (age undisclosed[3]) reject Islam (as well as Christianity, it should be noted) because they claim to be bullied and picked on by Asian boys at school. Jake is so unhappy, we are told, that he chooses to move to another 'more balanced' mixed school much further away than his present one; a school where there is greater diversity in the ethnic mix of pupils, and where the proportion of white kids is higher.

This story presents an apposite example of the ways in which the local and the personal are mobilized in debates over definitions of national identity and national culture. The documentary was filmed in Bradford which, as one commentator noted, 'has come to symbolise the bruised state of race relations in this country' (Manzoor 2003). Amongst other events that led Bradford to be marked as an area of 'racial tension',[4] it was one of three northern English towns where, in the summer of 2001, violent street-uprisings shook the nation and led to public debates about the promises and failures of multiculturalism. The subsequent *Cantle Report* (Home Office 2001a), produced by a government inquiry into the causes of the riots, will be discussed below.

What interests me here is how the film was taken up in the press as a symptom of the state of the nation, be it 'bruised' or 'confused but successful[ly] integrat[ed]' (Lappin 2003). It is worth noting that the myth surrounding the documentary form is that it makes truth claims that other audio-visual forms, such as the soap opera, for example, do not. Certainly, soaps blur the distinction between fiction and 'the real' and thus also make truth claims about the state of the 'real' world. What is specific to the documentary, however, is that it interpellates viewers to witness an *already given* reality (this is how it *is*), represented through a non-fictively performed narrative. In the case discussed here, the film 'documents' what happens to white children growing up in an ostensibly 'non-white' world. As an 'account' of children's complex affective reactions in their quest for belonging and friendship, the documentary called upon its viewers to think about the limits of national toleration as it ostensibly revealed what is likely to happen if 'multiculture' is not properly managed, thus tapping into the national nightmare of who 'we' might become.

The film was variously received by the press and the wider public. For some it sounded an alarming warning bell against the threats posed by too much exposure to 'other' cultures in schools and neighbourhoods where whites are outnumbered. Others welcomed the film for addressing 'the taboo subject of racism against white people' (Shaw 2003). In contrast, some commentators were 'intrigued' or 'fascinated' by the Gallagher girls' skills in adopting Islamic practices and at crossing the cultural borders drawn between Pakistani and English neighbours, and praised the girls for offering some hope for a 'confused' but 'vaguely encouraging' future (Lappin 2003; also I. Millar 2003). Overall, whatever the viewpoint, the personal and local forms of closeness viewers were called upon to witness were making local daily life a national affair, raising anxieties or hope about the future of Britain's white children, but also of all Britons/Britain, in the portrayal of the gradual Islamicization of the nation's daughters. In other words, a national drama was played out through the portrayal of the immediate experience of inter-ethnic propinquity.

What caught the attention of reviewers and what distinguished *The Last White Kids* from numerous other documentaries about multicultural Britain – which centre predominantly on ethno-racial minorities' negotiation of and integration within Britain and Britishness – is that a white English family is cast as the minority, and, moreover, young white girls are converting to Islam. The collective *frisson* provoked by the girls' conversion reverberates within a society haunted by colonial fears about miscegenation and the preservation of white femininity as the marker of the boundaries and property rights of nation and Empire (Anthias and Yuval-Davis 1989; McClintock 1995; Ware 1992; Young 1995). What interests me is the historical specificity of the anxiety as it is projected onto the young white Muslim convert living in northern England, and the implications of this in relation to the changing British multicultural landscape, namely with respect to the consolidation of religion as the privileged marker of radical and absolute difference since 11 September 2001.

This is not to say that anxieties about Islam did not exist prior to 9/11. The significance of political and social issues involving Muslims has been growing in Britain and in Europe since the late 1980s (Hussain and Miller 2006; Modood 2005; Modood *et al.* 2005) and with them, concerns about Islamophobia (Runnymede Trust 1997). In Britain, the Rushdie Affair of the late 1980s was a key moment in shifting the focus onto religious faith within political debates about multiculture. This was amplified in subsequent disturbances in Bradford (see note 4), and most recently, in the summer of 2001. Concerns about the seductiveness of Islam were further heightened and have acquired a special significance in the post-9/11 'war on terror' waged in the name of civilization. It is with these historical legacies in mind that I consider how *The Last White Kids* (filmed and broadcast before 7/7) concerns wider issues of the categories and location of closeness and distance, and the organization of multiple identities and identification, in a changing multicultural landscape. How can we understand the gendered differences between the girls' attraction to Islam, and the boys' rebuff? How can we understand some reviewers' alarmed responses to the girls' lives? How do they relate to wider fears about loss of national self?

This chapter examines how some forms of 'multicultural intimacy' are imagined through a *politics of inter-ethnic propinquity*. Within popular and policy discourses, different versions of multiculturalism co-exist that assume different types of intimacy – some assimilationist, some differentialist, some sexual, some platonic. Thus we need to differentiate spaces and scales in which 'intimacies' occur, or in which they are deployed conceptually. My focus on propinquity here is meant to capture the ways in which popular and policy discourses position inter-ethnic relationships between Muslim Asians[5] and white English people in the field of propinquity rather than that of personal intimacy. The term propinquity is particularly apposite as it denotes 'nearness in space; proximity; close kinship; similarity' (OED). It thus captures how ideals of proximity and similarity may at once be distinct from and slide into notions of kinship, but with an implied assumption of non-erotic intimacy. While notions of similarity can be easily conceived in terms of family resemblance – 'close kinship' – they are also understood as nearness. Propinquity is about neighbourliness which, as Michael Sorkin points out, is 'the ground and problem of democracy' (1999: 4). Indeed, city politics are:

> deeply inscribed in questions of propinquity and access, in the legibility and tractability of routines of circulation and contact: the *currency* of propinquity is exchange, the most vital measure of the city's intensity.
>
> (Sorkin 1999: 4; emphasis original)

Such a politics is at the heart of the decidedly localized understanding of 'community cohesion' found in policy discourse that presupposes that 'meaningful' inter-ethnic mixing (Home Office 2001a: 9) cannot occur without spatial and physical proximity. Yet concealed within a generalized 'inter-ethnicness' are several conditions that prescribe who can mix with whom and under what circumstances.

If, as established in Chapter 1, racial, ethnic, and cultural relations are imagined through specific emotional and ethical injunctions, such as loving thy neighbour, these injunctions are also imagined in the ambivalent spatial terms of *obligations to* and *dangers of* proximity. In this sense, the politics of inter-ethnic propinquity are both about physical relations in geographically bounded areas, as well as about the conception of non-physical relationships in terms of a spatial social imaginary. This is exemplified in the decidedly localized understanding of 'community cohesion' found in policy discourse, which presupposes that inter-ethnic mixing cannot occur without spatial and physical proximity, or in New Labour's investment in neighbourhoods as the ideal sites for activating engaged citizenship and a sense of identity and belonging for local residents (e.g. Office of the Deputy Prime Minister 2005). Indeed, the British government's faith in community cohesion was formulated in the aftermath of the 2001 riots, as I explain below, and was founded in concerns about distance and closeness between neighbouring communities within a given area. New forms of intimacy, of 'being together', were thus invested in ideas of 'community cohesion' and their related technologies of corrective citizenship which were proposed in order to groom men and women into proper citizens of multicultural Britain.

Thus the neighbourhood is targeted in national social policies as a contained, scaled-down unit that has its own demographic characteristics. Sometimes this translates into an ethnic- and/or class-mapping of the national space which suggests *both* disjuncture and unity between locality and the nation. That is, neighbourhoods are conceived as unique or different in terms of class and, most often, (multi)ethnic make-up, and situated somewhat outside of the nation, while at the same time they are seen as constitutive of, and resulting from, national diversity and tolerance. This also points to how the politics of inter-ethnic propinquity attempt to define the *contents* of practices *within* various scalar units that constitute the national: women can wear the hijab at home, but should not in schools or when meeting with their MP; women and their children must speak English at home as well as in the streets (Blunkett 2002); guidelines about the right proportion of mixing in schools, in housing estates, or in local politics and community organizations (Home Office 2001a). With regard to our immediate concerns then, which kinds of propinquity are celebrated and which are pathologized and deemed to be in need of correction? And how are these framed in terms of good neighbourliness? Far from condoning all forms of inter-ethnic propinquity, 'mixing' is framed within a tight policing of community relations. In this sense, the imperative of loving thy neighbour refers to both the desires for, and anxieties about, what the 'embrace' stems from and fosters. *Who mixes with whom and under what circumstances, is not left to chance.* Moreover, who can love whom is not only inflected by ethnicity but is further complicated by, and refracted through, class and gendered differentiations of masculinity and femininity, as will become clear below. Thus I examine the implications of prescriptions of good neighbourliness that gloss over the conflicts, tensions, inequalities, and power relations that are constitutive of 'living with difference' in deprived areas.

One might wonder how and why we have moved from a television documentary to social policy. By putting these in dialogue with each other, I draw out various senses of the nation as they are conveyed through imaginings of acceptable 'mixing' and good neighbourliness. As Gail Lewis argues, social policy documents 'are texts that aim to lay out a problem of governance and suggest ways in which that problem might be managed or resolved. As texts they are forms of representation in which a relation between objects and subjects is constituted' (2005: 537). Moreover, reports on community cohesion following the 2001 civil unrests were widely covered in the national press and much heed was paid to the proposed strategies of inter-ethnic mixing. If, as I document below, 'mixing' became a privileged technology of governance to address issues of segregation, fear, and mutual suspicion, it also circulated widely in the public domain as *the* truth about the problems of multiculturalism. In this sense, technologies not only regulate or dictate individual behaviours, but are apparatuses of discourse which account 'for the ways that knowledge is both constructed and imparted' (Kamboureli 1998: 210; also de Lauretis 1987). Technologies of 'mixing' geared towards the management of inter-ethnic propinquity, then, are invested with, but also construct specific ideas about, how people (should) relate to each other and live peacefully side-by-side. By going to the way of seeing that policy and televisual texts such as *The Last White Kids* open up, my aim is to attend to the ways in which both policy and popular discourses 'figure social life in certain imaginary ways' (Butler 2002: 28) that would exemplify the kind of coherence that is expected from individuals in their daily lives. That is, how national cohesion is figured in localized, personalized relationships, and conceived in terms of how people have to make decisions and choices around the control over their feelings and their relationships, and about their identities/identifications as if these were discrete entities. But more than that, I also consider the incommensurability of people's lives and social or public discourses about them by counterposing my own reading of *The Last White Kids* – not as the 'truth' about their lives, nor because I believe in the transparency of this or any other narrative; no narrative of self is transparent. Rather, by counterposing my reading against policy and popular texts I am suggesting, in accordance with Gail Lewis (2005: 538), that there is a whole range of experiences, feelings, and opinions that policy frameworks, as well as popular representations and conceptions, simultaneously produce and occlude for those who are positioned as variously minoritized subjects. The politics of propinquity seek to monitor and are founded on *legible* adjacencies, *intelligible* exchange – the currency of propinquity – the limits of which are continuously challenged in the mundane, messy, unorthodox forms of daily encounter. In this sense, *The Last White Kids* could be seen as a ground for multiple displacements and translations that the programmatic structure of good neighbourliness cannot, or refuses to, accommodate.

The promise of mixing

It is in the wake of uprisings in Oldham, Burnley, and Bradford between May and July 2001 that a new politics of inter-ethnic propinquity became imperative – one which emphasized inter-ethnic interactions and mixing as the pathway to integration. Widely reported as 'race riots', the 2001 'summer of violence' shook the nation into self-examination about its track record in multicultural management. The riots involved large numbers of people from different backgrounds – especially young men – and resulted in the destruction of property and attacks on individuals. The confrontations were largely between Asian youths and the police, and were prompted by racist groups, including the BNP, attacking Asian individuals and communities, and by 'the failure of the police to provide protection from this threat' (Kundnani 2001: 105). Local and national enquiries were set up to investigate the causes of the riots. Three local reports were produced

(Burnley Task Force 2001; Oldham Independent Review 2001; Ouseley 2001), while the Home Office set up a Ministerial Group on Public Order and Community Cohesion (see Home Office 2001b), as well as an independent review team led by Ted Cantle (Home Office 2001a; also known as the Cantle Report), to identify ways to promote better 'community cohesion' at national policy level as well as in local governments and in local communities themselves. The Cantle Report, with its 'local community cohesion plan' and its sixty-seven practical measures to '"mainstream" the process of community cohesion' (Home Office 2001a: 11), laid the foundations for subsequent government strategies and initiatives aimed at promoting community cohesion and racial equality. Ted Cantle is regarded as the 'founding father' of community cohesion in Britain (Benjamin 2005) and he has been associated with those who have sounded the death knell of multiculturalism on the basis of a narrow definition that associates it with segregationist identity politics and practices.

All reports about the disturbances agreed that ethnic segregation was a root-cause of the violence and recommended mixing as a pathway to integration – especially in schools, but also outside schools and in the fabric of the local community. The rationale is that children will learn toleration through mixing with 'others', and thus become good moral citizens. The Cantle Report recommended that: 'Even where pupils are from mixed ethnic backgrounds, if they live in segregated housing they will need to be encouraged to mix outside of school ... Besides encouraging children to mix with each other this has to be extended to include parents as well' (Home Office 2001a: 17). In an interview for the *Guardian*, Cantle subsequently reiterated 'how important it is that kids meet not just at school but that parental networks and friendship patterns are absolutely vital' (Benjamin 2005). Concerns arose from all corners about 'communities operat[ing] on the basis of a series of parallel lives. These lives often do not seem to touch at any point, let alone overlap and promote any *meaningful interchanges*' (Home Office 2001a: 9; emphasis added). Children and their parents were specifically encouraged to cross their neighbours' threshold and to literally 'visit their respective homes, for instance, for a birthday party' (Home Office 2001a: 17). This, in the Cantle Report's view, will facilitate recognition and, crucially, the emergence of community cohesion.

The Cantle Report marked the institutionalization of 'mixing' as a key governing principle for the management of inter-ethnic propinquity in local communities across the country. 'Mixing' was widely hailed as the antidote to segregation, disaffection, distrust, hate and fear, all of which result from too much sameness. It is noticeable that for all the discussions about racism available in the plethora of Home Office documents about community cohesion (albeit a racism reductively understood as barely anything more than the consequence of ignorance or jealousy, which in turn, are seen as resulting from economic deprivation), what has dominated public debates since 2001 is the issue of *ethnic* segregation and separation.

The Cantle Report and others concede that an important role is played by 'settled' ethnic communities in supporting new immigrants or those who are economically deprived (Home Office 2001a: 59; also Home Office 2003), and a subsequent Home Office consultation document agreed that mono-ethnic propinquity 'is not in itself a sign of a breakdown in cohesion' (Home Office 2004a: 16). Still, 'ethnic' community cohesion has been consistently and generally singled out and the overwhelming view remains that 'it is possible to find social cohesion within increasingly divided neighbourhoods. Individuals may well be well integrated into their local *ethnic or religious-based communities*, which then *creates divisions* between these communities and others' (Home Office 2001a: 70; emphasis added). The accepted understanding is that, due to mutual fear, suspicion, or plain ignorance, 'different *ethnic* groups are increasingly segregating themselves from each other and retreating into "comfort zones" made up of people like themselves' (Ouseley 2001: 16; emphasis added). This 'self-segregation' is seen by some in the Home Office as 'something which successive groups of *immigrants* have done for centuries' (Home Office 2001b: 12; emphasis added). However, this kind of 'cohesion' hinders the version of cohesion favoured by the national government: 'social cohesion requires that participation extends *across* the confines of local communities, knitting them together into a wider whole' (Ferlander and Timms in Home Office 2001a: 70; emphasis added). It 'is about helping micro-communities to gel or mesh into an integrated whole' (Home Office 2001a: 70). Framed within a politics of toleration, the key aim of this version of multiculturalism is 'to promote racial harmony *between* communities, [while] it fails to deal with problems *within* communities' (such as forced marriage) (Southall Black Sisters in Razack 2004: 166; emphasis SBS).

In a consultation document about community cohesion and racial equality circulated to local governments in May 2004, the Home Office wrote of the importance of addressing the common problems between groups constituting a 'community', while neglecting to consider internal problems within groups whose 'culture' and 'traditions' merit recognition.

> [I]t is important that we foster mutual understanding and respect between people from different backgrounds and cultures. Communities are better equipped to organise themselves and tackle problems if they are not divided by mutual suspicion and misunderstanding of diverse cultures and faiths. We need to understand better why segregation persists in some of our communities – so we can ensure people do not feel forced into it, while respecting their right to retain their culture and tradition.
>
> (Home Office 2004a: 16–17)

This way of posing 'multiculture' indicates that 'mixing' is about holding cultural boundaries tight, locked, and then talking across them – a 'dialogical mosaic' (Hesse 2000: 8). Furthermore, this statement locates and contains 'culture' and 'traditions' within ethnic communities. Within neo-liberal moral racist politics discussed in Chapter 1, where the 'glue of values' (Goodhart 2004) constitute the national bond, culture and traditions are increasingly privatized as an 'ethnic' issue that does not concern the national. This version of multiculturalism does not go 'beyond the wall of language' (Žižek 1998: 168) and keeps the other at a distance, enclosed within her culture – the Muslim Asian other, that is, for this version of mixing is different to those of the younger generation 'Caribbeans' who are mixing/mixed in a different sense. Hence the generalization of 'ethnic minorities' and 'immigrants' in the citations above elides some of the specific issues faced by various groups residing in given areas – including the white English – while it produces a significant erasure of the different conditions under which peoples migrate, settle, and live in England. More specifically, the erasure of 'Pakistanis', 'Asians', 'Muslims', who are the main minoritized groups concerned here, raises several questions about what is denied or made visible regarding their specific integration strategies. Can the experience of South Asians and Caribbean people be aligned to each other? And how does religion play out here? These and other questions[6] reach beyond the scope of this chapter, but one point of entry is an analysis of how, within this generalized conception of 'inter-ethnicness' where all types of mixings are celebrated, there lies an implicit distinction between sexual and cultural reproduction, as well as an implicit fusion of the 'interracial' into the 'inter-ethnic'. We glimpsed this distinction in the previous chapter. I further unveil it in the next section, namely with regard to Devlin, the Gallagher girls' mixed-race cousin, and his (self) portrayal in the film – as black and not black, and as decidedly not Pakistani Muslim. In addition, the question of who can embrace whom is not only inflected by ethnicity and race, but is further refracted through class and gendered differentiations of masculinity and femininity, as *The Last White Kids* shows. But first, it is worth considering some of the issues at stake in framing the challenge of mixing in terms of ethnic segregation. Two inter-related matters arise: the excessive presence and absence of Muslims and the proposed redress of this situation through balance and the severance of diasporic belongings.

The issue of getting the right mix is about striking the right balance. Arguing that he is not an assimilationist, Cantle has stated that it is important to respect and 'preserve cultural identities, which means you need a critical mass of different people in an area to support separate shops, temples or mosques. The problem is when that becomes total exclusion' (Benjamin 2005). To avoid 'total exclusion', the Cantle Report recommended (and Cantle reiterated in Benjamin 2005) quotas in faith-based schools (among other things) whereby they should offer 'at least 25% of places to other faiths or denominations and would immediately be more inclusive and create a better representation of all cultures or ethnicities'

(Home Office 2001a: 37).[7] The problem, in other words, is when there is not a 'balanced' mixing on the part of minorities.

The Last White Kids confronts its viewers with the excessive presence of the other. Muslims are too many and too close, constituted as *out-of-place* because *disproportionately* 'here', in the fullness of their existence which exceeds imaginings and representations of what constitutes 'balanced' mixing. Jake Gallagher's apparent decision to change school in favour of one where there is a 'more balanced' (Matthew 2003) mix, feeds into the perception of the excessive presence of undesirable others – the implication being that there is an excessive absence of whites. Only at the end of the documentary does it emerge that Jake is actually in his final year of primary education and that he would have changed schools anyway. Though the basis of his choice of school remains telling – his choice means a longer travelling time to school – the film and its reviewers mislead us into thinking that Jake's discomfort was so high that he was willing to change school during his primary education.

The film is taken as emblematic of the multicultural nightmare where disproportionate diversity of the wrong kind undermines social cohesion by taking white English people away from what is perceived as 'their' community. The apparent 'exclusiveness' of the Muslims in Manningham, and the excessive interest expressed by the Gallagher girls towards their Muslim neighbours, are seen by several reviewers as evidence of the loss of national cohesion and direction. We can recall David Goodhart's concerns, discussed in Chapter 1, that tolerance is undermining commitment to and care for the national community because 'we [the UK] don't care enough about each other to resent the arrival of the other' (2004: 25). Viewers are asked to witness the loss of social cohesion within the community as the girls are being pulled away from a version of national community cohesion that is not simply about national *identity*, but rather about *identification* with and attachment to the British nation and its citizens.

Thus, *The Last White Kids* is situated within a set of wider issues about category, power, locations of affect/distance, and the organization of (multiple) identities and identifications in such ways that *one* is the nodal point – and it must be the 'right' one. It is useful, in this respect, to return to Laclau and Mouffe's (1985) concept of the 'nodal point'[8] for it captures the ways in which discourses are always constituted as an attempt to arrest the flows of differences. Nodal points are points of 'partial fixation' of meaning that derive from the very openness and indeterminacy of meanings and practices. The nation, in this respect, is nothing more than the articulation of nodal points insofar as 'nation' is impossible – 'it cannot simply be the expression of something already acquired' (Laclau and Mouffe 1985: 113–14), nor can it wholly subsume differences and fully represent its constitutive parts. Thus the problems of governance concern the modalities of connections across difference scales. In other words, the problems of managing multiculture are about how people move across scales, how connections are made, and how that movement and those connections can be controlled and contained. The national fantasy, in this respect, is the fantasy of containing multi-local connections within one single, national, domestic space of belonging and identification.

Crucial to community cohesion is the 'intertwining of personal and place identity' (Home Office 2001a: 13), but where the 'place' of identity is *here* not 'there'. The ideal of a local cohesive community is grounded in the attempt to shift cultural identities, identifications, and practices of local residents, especially those of minorities who must break away from their 'self-segregated' communities (Kundnani 2001: 107). 'Ethnic' (read Asian, Pakistani, or Muslim) self-love is dismissed as a form of schizophrenic self-ostracism, a kind of make-believe world where children of ethnic minorities are 'being raised and schooled in an environment where they can forget that in the world outside Manningham it is they who are the real ethnic minority', as one reviewer of *The Last White Kids* stated (Manzoor 2003). While she is kept at a distance – we don't want too much of you, nor should you be too close – the Muslim Asian is also expected to 'care back' in the relationship of neighbourly love. Cohesive communities are 'caring communities' which are scrutinized in relation to the injunctions of caring citizenship that come with them – that is the expectation that citizens should '"care back" through their active and affective participation in the nation' (Hage 2003: 30). Viewed in this light, can the 'problem' of Muslim Asian perceived self-segregation be the problem of their refusal of the love and embrace offered by the nation; of their refusal to 'care back'? *Love of the same is undesirable when it is not about 'us'.* This gives a different twist to the politics of recognition discussed by Charles Taylor (1994), which seeks to redress the injuries of misrecognition suffered by minorities. Here, the injured is the white English subject and the wider local/national community whose offer of friendship, respect, and tolerance with intimacy is rebuffed by a seemingly un-neighbourly ethnic minority. Such a scenario was decidedly at the centre of *The Last White Kids*, where Muslims are represented as assimilating white Christian Britain without concession to its values and culture. On the basis of their assumed fixed, unilateral, and homogeneous identity, the onus is put on ethnic minorities to cross over and meet their neighbours in a relation of pseudo-mutual recognition.

Of central concern are outer-local attachments that diasporic communities might foster.

> Britain, like almost all countries, has been affected by globalisation and is now host to communities for whom concerns about their country of origin can be refreshed daily. In these circumstances, strategies for making them feel at home, rather than as reluctant exiles, need to be established.
>
> (Home Office 2001a: 18)

Still founded in ideas of location as geographically grounded in a singular and geographically bounded locale, technologies of governance aimed at fostering inter-ethnic neighbourliness fail in the face of challenges posed by contemporary social practices of the virtual and the transnational that give different grounds of belonging or identification. The problem of governance here is the problem of achieving a sustainable inter-ethnic propinquity at a time when cohesion is perceived as threatened by perceived unilateral 'outside belongings'.[9] With diaspora's impetus to be located outside of the boundaries of the nation, a crisis might emerge between multiculturalism and nation *through* diaspora. Diasporic formations are 'both cartographic and dispositional' (Hesse 2000: 21); that is that they describe geographical contours of dispersal 'of particular communities from a historical place of domicile to geographically different places of generational settlement' (Hesse 2000: 20) within and across national borders. At the same time, diaspora formations also refer to transnational 'elective affinities' (Hesse 1999, 2000) that animate certain communities or individuals who imagine themselves as part of a diaspora. The resounding silence and absence of Muslims and Pakistanis in the streets where the Gallagher children are seen to roam epitomizes the image of the absent-present immigrant. The one whose transnational liaisons – the presence of which are made visible and audible in the local mosque – take her outside of the locality into a transnational diasporic space of belonging. This suggests an excess in the other direction to the one discussed above: if the Muslim Asian is out of place because there is 'too much' of her and she is 'too close', she is also *out* of place because she is not here *though she should be*. She is eerily invisible and unavailable for participating in neighbourly 'meaningful interchanges' and for loosing herself into 'us'.

For the Cantle Report, of central concern in fostering place-attachment for new British citizens and permanent residents is defining 'what it means to be a citizen of a modern multi-racial Britain', where there is no room for looking 'backwards to some supposedly halcyon days of a mono-cultural society, or alternatively look[ing] to [another] country of origin for some form of identity' (Home Office 2001a: 9).

> [M]any of the young people, and those that work with them, have stressed their desire to break down the barriers between different groups in the community and to work together to build a harmonious future. For many of them, a priority is to control troublemakers, most of whom come into the area from outside. They also hope for changes in parental attitudes where they seem to want to cling to some past life, perhaps one left behind in their country of origin.
>
> (Home Office 2001a: 18)

'[T]roublemakers' coming 'from outside' – such as the BNP or other racist organizations – and immigrants' attachments to 'some past life' are cast as equally disruptive to local cohesion. Aligned on a system of equivalence, racists, far-right nationalists and immigrants are linked together as obstacles to the achievement of community cohesion. All are equally guilty in looking backwards rather than forwards – be it back to an imagined homogeneous white Britain, or back to the 'old' country. Lumped together, the white and Asian poor of inner city areas are seen as exhibiting a 'poverty of identity based on outdated ways of thinking and being' (Haylett 2001: 352).

We are moving, here, between different registers of inter-ethnic propinquity and these registers are cast in terms of different spatio-temporal horizons: the problem of dealing with *local* domestic affective spheres of belonging that are anachronistic, monocultural and/or transnational, and the project of creating a *national multicultural* domestic space. National feeling is perceived as hindered by transnational/monocultural attachments and the project is to realign personal feelings, feelings for the community, and feelings for the (multicultural) nation on the same continuum. The project of multicultural Britain seeks to contain local households and communities within one national domestic space of multicultural intimacy. Migrants' detachment from their roots is seen as a necessary condition to the process of establishing strong local ties: 'cling[ing] to some past life' (Home Office, 2001a: 18), or 'the burden of "back home" politics' (Home Office 2001a: 20) are discouraged as counterproductive to community cohesion.

Furthermore, the balanced presence expected of ethnic minorities relates to discourses of intimate good neighbourliness captured in the Cantle Report's appeal for loving thy neighbour cited in the epigraph. Indeed, at the foundation of ideals of the good community is the good neighbour, whereby individuals are constituted through the social relations of neighbourliness in which they are embedded.

(The) becoming neighbour

Sharon Gallagher and her neighbours are living in a relationship of genial indifference, which is fragile and at times grudging. In the only neighbourly interaction shown in the film, we see Sharon Gallagher in her back yard, holding a neighbour's newborn baby, doting over her, trying in vein to pronounce her name. In another scene, she mechanically lists her neighbours by ethnic background (describing one as 'Asian but she speaks like me'), while in a third scene she expresses her disapproval at hearing an imam calling her daughter Aisha rather than Ashlene. Sharon Gallagher's prosaic negotiations with her neighbours reveal the multifaceted nature of living with difference, where desire, tolerance, and unease intermingle. All in all, however, Sharon Gallagher is portrayed as having accommodated to her neighbourhood, but with inappropriate apathy. That is, an insistent tone of concern overshadows the documentary so that viewers overlook the matter-of-factness of Sharon's views about her and her children's experience, and are rather incredulous of her when she says she has 'no problems' with her neighbours.[10]

Living side-by-side, rather than face-to-face, Sharon Gallagher and her neighbours engage in what could be read as an ethical relation of indifference (Sandercock 2003; Tonkiss 2003), one where there is no attempt to cross the neighbour's threshold and have the 'meaningful interchanges' prescribed by the Home Office (Home Office 2001a: 9). Sharon Gallagher's outlook resembles the blasé attitude to difference, an attitude usually attributed to city-life, indeed seen as an inherent factor when living among strangers in the metropolis (Donald, 1999; Sandercock 2003; Sennett 1994; Simmel 1997). Though Bradford is not a 'world city', it has grown to become emblematic of the 'state of race relations in this country' (Manzoor 2003), as explained above. Certainly, the propinquity of Asianness and Englishness in Bradford exists under different conditions to that of Asians and English in London or Manchester, and creates variations on the structures of feeling that encourage neighbourly love. Bradford is one of several deprived towns and areas that have become the targets for strategies of capacity-building, community cohesion, active citizenship, and multicultural management. It is an area where residents struggle for material recognition and resources – Sharon Gallagher waited 18 months for her council home – and where anti-Asian antagonism is in part grounded on perceptions of Asians' luxurious lifestyles as proof of preferential treatment; a racism based on consumer rather than ethnic culture. But the point is that this story is overshadowed by a sense that Manningham is not a 'good community', but rather a 'failed community ... where neighbours appear as if they are strangers to each other' (Ahmed 2000: 26) which is construed as a consequence of the unbalanced mixing between such radically different cultures.

The failure is measured against prescriptions of good neighbourliness whereby 'love rather than genial indifference sets the standard and it is, after all, only the neighbour and not the more demanding figures of the enemy or the stranger, who is being brought within the sphere of this impossible request for tolerance with intimacy' (Gilroy 2004a: 72). The request for tolerance with intimacy is impossible because it sets up injunctions of love and understanding that neglect the relations of distance, power, and conflict that living with difference is embedded in. The illusion of tolerance with multicultural intimacy is that power relations and conflicts will be somehow suspended through intimacy, and that the distance and hierarchy between those who tolerate and those who are tolerated will dissolve.

Furthermore, the enemy or stranger is not necessarily as distinct from the neighbour as Gilroy suggests. The sophistication and detailed guidelines of how community cohesion can be attained suggests that 'the neighbour' itself is an achieved rather than a given status. 'What makes for good neighbours' was a topic of study in the Home Office's proposed training programme for applicants for British naturalization (Home Office 2003: 10), and is implicit throughout another document on *Why Neighbour-hoods Matter* (Office of the Deputy Prime Minister 2005). The belief in the benefits of neighbourly love comes with the acknowledgment that 'thy neighbour' must *gain* 'thy love' through appropriate behaviour. The Blair government's Anti-Social Behaviour Act 2003 and Respect Agenda laun-ched in 2006 are examples. Both aim at tackling anti-social behaviour, defined as including a range of behaviours from 'nuisance neighbours' [sic], to 'yobbish behaviour', 'graffiti', or 'reckless driving of mini-motorbikes' – behaviours that have been repeatedly associated with working-class youths. On the anti-social behaviour page of the respect.gov.uk website, a photo-graph appears at the top. It is of four youths wearing 'hoodies' (hooded sweatshirts), standing in front of a closed storefront and talking, two of them holding a canned drink, the nature of which is unclear. Two of them also have their arms stretched out and their hands touching, as if exchan-ging a small item – a joint? a coin? a cigarette? a piece of paper? Moving the cursor to the photo, a small window appears bearing the message: 'asb [anti-social behaviour] hanging around'.[11] Nothing in the photograph indicates that these youths are a nuisance. It is consistent, however, with the demonization of working-class 'chav' youth as threat and, as such, as the privileged target in community policing and technologies of corrective citizenship aimed at preserving good neighbourliness and social cohesion.

Thus the very location in which *The Last White Kids* is set is not inno-cent: this is a working-class neighbourhood in a northern English town – where the white English working-class poor are imagined as hopeless monoculturalists, racists, and anti-social (Haylett 2001; Skeggs 2004). This is exemplified in the film by the Gallagher boys' exhibition of indifference or contempt for their Muslim neighbours. Jake, filmed walking the streets in his hoody, explains his lack of interest in Islam because Islam means having 'to go to the mosque about a million times a day', to learn 'all that reading backwards', and 'you'd miss the Simpsons'. The boy is concerned with keeping his daily routine intact; a day that would be devoid of *any* religious obligation – Jake also rejects Christianity, a point that no reviewer picked up on, while only one noted cousin Lauren's remark about her brother John calling Jesus 'a hairy bastard' (Lappin 2003). Instead, the boys' defiant behaviour is construed in the film as caused by the excessive presence of Muslim Asians who refuse to mix and whose boys are bullying the now victimized and minoritized white kids – Jake recalls being called a 'white bastard' and his mother, 'a prostitute', at school. Assuming that bullying might very well be going on, the Gallagher boys' attitude should rather be read as part of wider 'patterns of embodied masculine culture that they share with their [Asian] peers' (Desai in Back *et al.* 2002: 5.4). Both Asian and white boys of Manningham are 'all too well assimilated into a society divided by racism and discrimination' (Back *et al.* 2002: 5.4), and into an insecure post-industrial society. Indeed, for many young working-class men, the meaning of masculinity is in transition, and must be defined outside of industrial labour. As Anoop Nayak argues, the exhibition of the 'spectacular masculinity' of male excess might be a means of accruing 'body capital that has a currency and a local exchange value within the circuits they inhabit' (2006: 813). The alleged school playground fights between the Gallagher boys and their Pakistani peers could be an enactment of muscular masculinity within a competition over street credibility and control. But rather than situating the boys' violence within a historical and social understanding of race and class interactions and confrontations, racism here is reduced to a question of individual 'bad faith' and 'bad practice'. The Gallagher boys and their Asian peers are all seen as failing integration because they engaged in the unacceptable working-class yobbery that shames the nation and that has become the target of increased scrutiny, regulation, and control.

However, if the boys' violence calls for a rethinking of racism as historical, rather than merely individual, their attitude toward cultural difference also points to the very ambivalence of racial thinking. While they insist on the impermeability of ethnic categories and indeed act in defence of them, they also force a reconsideration of the black/white binary. Consider the filmmaker Shona Thompson's question to Devlin about why he fights with the Asian kids: 'But they're the same people as you, aren't they?' she asked while pointing out their similar skin colour. But Devlin adamantly rejects the connection, privileging his filial ties to his white brother John instead, and declaring 'I'm a Porkie, not a Paki'. Choosing to fight Islam and Pakistanis rather than to relate to them as a black boy, Devlin rejects what Gayatri Spivak calls 'chromatism' (in McClintock 1995: 52) – where skin colour is the crucial sign of otherness and belonging – and repositions himself within a neo-racist scale – one that places religion, rather than skin colour, as the primary criteria of absolute difference. Devlin might well refuse to be 'black' in the same way his Asian peers are, but he resorts to a cultural absolutist and familyist discourse of blood ties to assert his inherent 'difference' from Muslims, as well as his assimilation within white England.

In contemporary Britain, policy and popular rhetoric distinguish between 'settled communities' of the 'old' migration (Black Caribbean and South Asians), on the one hand, and 'new' faith-based communities or 'new' migrants (East European work permit holders, asylum-seekers from Afghanistan or Iraq), on the other. As Gail Lewis agues, this 'points to ... the *particular* problematic of producing a new black or Asian subject whose primary or transcendent identification is with the nation(al)' (Lewis 2006b: 345; emphasis original). But as Thompson's interaction with Devlin reveals, the black Caribbean subject is simultaneously denied full belonging through the very process of minoritization. Devlin's emphatic refusal to be 'one of them' speaks to his own struggle to be *of* the white English community and *of* the nation, rather than of a 'settled community' or 'ethnic minority' that is always already a guest in the 'host' nation's home.

Seen as assimilated yet violent, we could also wonder if Devlin's 'half-Jamaicanness' doesn't enter in full force here, given that Jamaican men have long since been symbols par excellence of masculine violence and crime (the 'Yardie'). What would it mean for him to say, like his sister Lauren cited below, that he is 'in the middle'? This raises questions that I cannot begin to answer, but the point is that there are several different types of mixing and 'integration' that question the foundations of racial thinking, while they can also simultaneously reinforce existing categorizations (Ali 2003: 18).[12] Thompson's attempt to slot Devlin within a black/white divide fails in the face of an ambivalent racism that ostensibly places more emphasis on what you are 'at heart' than on skin colour. Moreover, Devlin embodies that version of multicultural intimacy that is about sexual reproduction and assimilation of black Caribbeanness into white Britain – a version that is taken for granted in contrast to the question of mixing as it is posed in the film, as well as in policy and popular discourses more generally. Within the generalized 'inter-ethnicness' where all types of proximity are celebrated or feared, there is an implicit fusion of the 'interracial' into the 'inter-ethnic' that conceals the different historical conditions of settlement, integration, and indeed 'mixing' experienced by different migrants and minorities, and that conceals the impact that these have on the positioning of minorities within the national landscape. In much of the policy and popular discourses, the assumption is that Asians, especially Muslims, constitute a single, separate, unitary 'ethnicity' whose members may occasionally cross the thresholds of local schools on organized visit days between faith-based schools, or the threshold of their neighours' homes, but who will not cross the sexual borders to form a 'mixed' household and family. The latter is more readily assumed of the black Caribbean subject, whose offspring are like Devlin (or Genevieve, of Chapter 3). When it comes to Islam, and by a sweeping generalization, Asians, intimacy is an issue of propinquity – geographical and cultural closeness, but one that does not breed sexually. The closeness with Muslim Asians is perceived as threatening because of a different kind of assimilation – one where Islam is seen as potentially annihilating white English daughters.

The Gallagher boys' insistence on the fixity of categories and on the impossibility of greeting their Asian peers with anything other than the same violence and aggression they say they are subjected to, stands in stark contrast to their sisters' behaviours. Ashlene and Amy regularly visit the local mosque. Ashlene is praised by the imam for her quick learning skills, and Amy astonishes the owner of a local pizza parlour when she flawlessly recites verses from the Koran. The girls obviously take pride in such attention and in such praise. Indeed, *this* is where they acquire street credibility, in contrast to the spectacular and muscular forms of masculinity exhibited by their brothers and cousins. With the scrutinizing lens cast on them, the Gallagher girls show the adaptability and flexibility of working-class white children who are performing acts of seamless syncretism usually associated with white middle-class civility and educated knowledge and/or with the ordinary cosmopolitanism of big urban centres. In doing so, the girls are breaking out of fixed notions of working-class culture and more broadly, of northern working-class towns and neighbourhoods. What *The Last White Kids* reveals, as Ash Amin suggests, is that the neighbourhood is a space of cultural displacement, where the girls disrupt 'easy labelling of the stranger as enemy and [initiate] new attachments . . . and through this, learn to become different through new patterns of social interaction' (2002: 970). For example, when asked by the filmmaker what religion she is, Lauren answers that she is 'in the middle'. 'You're not half Paki', retorts her brother John. 'I'm in the middle', insists Lauren with the only answer she can give within the rigid discursive system that is available to her; one that conflates 'ethnicity' and 'race' with religion, and that forces her to be *either* English-Christian *or* Pakistani-Muslim. Lauren exposes the limits of these categories, as they do not provide her with a satisfying way to express her own positioning within the multicultural horizon she inhabits. In this respect, the Gallagher girls offer some hope for the future by articulating a version of belonging that is not based on a foundational identity.

In another scene, Amy proudly displays a burkha and shows off her dexterity at putting it on. When asked why she would cover herself head-to-toe, she explains that it is because '[i]f you are white, no one can see your face, so they think you are Muslim'. In response, the two authors of the lengthiest review of the film, *Daily Mail*'s Sarah Chalmers and Chris Brooke (2003), despair that '[t]he image of any child feeling her natural looks are somehow inferior is especially poignant.' Though they note that Amy's and Ashlene's integration may be 'commendable', they add 'but they ARE the last white family in their Bradford street' (Chalmers and Brooke 2003). They continue:

> that two bright youngsters should take such an interest in the culture they find themselves immersed in, it [sic] is a phenomenon worthy of closer scrutiny, not least because it is likely to be mirrored elsewhere in Britain's inner cities.

The reviewers are not interested in the ways in which Amy and her sister are enacting different versions of femininity, nor can they see in Amy's remark a strategic play with the signifiers of inalterable difference. The prime issue of concern for Chalmers and Brooke is the minoritization of *white* English people *as white*, and Amy's explanation is taken up as a sign of the dangers of too much mixing of whites with otherness. In *The Last White Kids*, the Gallagher girls are seen as having lost a love of themselves as white; as having lost the very symbolic consistency of their being because they got too close to the 'other'. For these reviewers, the scene presents, in Anne Anlin Cheng's words, 'the real horror of an identificatory assimilation that has taken place *on the white body*' and expresses a 'usually unarticulated anxiety of the white self to remain unaffected'

(2001: 40; emphasis original) by its use of an iconic marker of otherness such as the veil. But Amy's remark says nothing of the feeling of inferiority perceived by Chalmers and Brooke. Her beaming face suggests more pride at her smart thinking, more self-possession than self-denial. Amy is fully aware of her being white, and of how white and Muslim don't quite add up in the world she lives in, and she is fully in control of what she does about her whiteness. The veil, here, simultaneously masks and confirms whiteness – Amy's whiteness is not under threat and she knows that she will always remain white. The veil is like a second skin that marks her as racialized other, but it is one that she can put on or remove at will.

If Amy uses the veil as a prop to pass as a Muslim girl, it is as a sign of authenticity that is also a disciplining technology. On the one hand, Amy and Ashlene adorn the veil as the required feminine vestment within the Muslim community they wish to join. By wearing the veil, they perform the kind of acceptable femininity required of them. On the other hand, the veil is also a disciplining technology used by non-Muslims against the Muslim population as a whole – we need only recall Jack Straw's infamous remark about women wearing the niqab as an example of the ways in which the veil is a privileged site for casting Muslims as failing national belonging (see next chapter). The elevation of the veil as *the* sign of threatening and oppressive gender orders airbrushes the ways in which technologies of gender and gender inequalities take on a myriad of forms and are not exclusive to Islam. In this sense, the kind of femininity and womanhood that the veil signifies in Britain is one that affronts an idealized view of the 'liberated' Western woman. The veil is the sign of an inferior sex/gender system and by the same token, confirms the superiority of the British (and European) 'more equal' sex/gender systems (Lewis 2006a; Razack 2004). Thus the portrayal of white British girls crossing the threshold of acceptable to unacceptable femininity becomes the sign of the crumbling of the nation's moral values. 'When will Britain convert to Islam?' shrieked Peter Hitchens in his *Mail on Sunday* headline (Hitchens 2003) that chimes with the BNP's alarmist rhetoric about the Islamicization of the UK.[13] In his review, the journalist expressed a deep concern about a younger generation bereft of proper patriarchal guidance as a result of 'the crumbling of two-parent families' (Sharon Gallagher is a single mother) and the waning leadership of white Christian churches, which consequently clears a space for imams to step in as patriarchal figures. Similarly, Chalmers and Brooke (2003) see the girls as 'victims of another largely Western phenomenon – the fatherless family. And it is clear from the documentary that they look to Muslim religious leaders for male approval.' The girls' interest in Islam becomes symbolic of that which is under threat by Islam, by the *possibility* of Islam (Ahmed 2004), a possibility that is associated by the *Daily Mail* and the *Mail on Sunday* with secularization and the decline of patriarchal authority. Racism and ethnic absolutism hide behind expressions of Christian patriarchy and 'the family' as being under siege, both of which are elevated as cornerstones of the morality of Britishness.

Without doubt, Ashlene's relationship to the mosque and the imam suggest that she finds there a parental type of caring and a kind of safety and assurance that give her the tools to blossom – her joy was palpable when her mother lifted a ban against her going to the mosque. However against a vision of annihilation such as the one conjured up by the *Mail on Sunday* and the *Daily Mail*, we can consider the mosque a safe space away from the streets where boys bully each other, where 'hanging around' can be seen as 'anti-social', and from where maybe several if not most of Ashlene's school friends are absent because they are themselves at the mosque. In this respect, safety counterbalances the 'fear' or threat of Muslim colonization and national destruction portrayed by reviewers (Hitchens 2003; Chalmers and Brook 2003). Ashlene and Amy also simply find in Islam a way to fit in and to beat the boredom of having no one to play with. As suggested above, theirs is a kind of border crossing that is organic to the very kind of place they live in; theirs is simply a strategy to fit in and to make friends.

Different sets of questions about crossing borders arise when Ashlene's search for safety is refracted through a generational femininity – not questions of racial and national integrity, but rather questions of gender and sexuality. When she returns to the mosque following her long absence, Ashlene was told to wait another month for a female teacher because, having reached the age of puberty, she could not longer be taught by her male teacher. Having crossed a generational threshold, Ashlene's movement across cultural borders is mediated by her gendered position. Now Ashlene has to be a different kind of girl – one whose burgeoning 'womanhood' positions her within sex/gender systems of inequalities that exist across 'ethnic' borders and that are at the basis of cross-ethnic complicities. Indeed, as stated above, in a political context where the prime concern is to promote racial harmony *between* communities, issues of gender (and class) inequalities and normative kinship systems within and across communities are neglected.[14]

So when they think of the well-integrated multicultural citizen, political leaders and commentators do not conjure up the image of the white English Muslim girl or woman, nor of the bullying, swearing angry Asian or white male youths, nor even of the indifferent resident. They do not conjure up the kinds of daily negotiations and practices that invariably challenge representational ideals of multicultural citizenry and the fantasy of national patriarchal hegemony. Rather, the politics of community cohesion and good neighbourliness are grounded in anxieties about 'race' that run deep in the national culture. What the film and its reviewers fail to consider is how messy, slippery, and fragile 'racial' differences actually are, how porous cultural boundaries can be, how fluid cultural practices are, and how experiences of racialized or culturalized differences are uneven across class, gender, and urban/regional divides (Lewis 2004b: 112).

Haunted by its potential failure to stabilize desirable forms of closeness, the management of inter-ethnic propinquity, then, seeks to build worlds and to create physical and emotional spaces by annexing and diverting unwanted kinds of relations, or by containing or subverting forms of attachments that exceed the organized and predictable forms that circulate in the public domain. Technologies of mixing 'have become sites of intense displacement for other political fears ... fears about new demographics, and about the very unity and transmitability of the nation' (Butler 2002: 21). Framed within a logic of balanced but engaged identification with the *here and now*, inter-ethnic propinquity is also invested with ideals of affective attachments that make good caring neighbours and good caring citizens. The promise of neighbourly love is to be viewed as part of a technology of governance aimed at achieving platonic intimacy with inter-ethnic propinquity. Such strategies not only concern, as Nigel Thrift (2004: 67) suggests, 'the careful design of urban space to produce political response' and action – such as 'linking projects' that bus children from all-Asian schools to all-white schools, and vice versa. The management of inter-ethnic propinquity is also constructed through specific emotional and ethical injunctions that are imagined in the ambivalent spatial terms of *obligations to* and *dangers of* proximity.

The Last White Kids stages failed inter-ethnic propinquity as viewers are invited to witness the Islamicization of the nation's unprotected daughters who roam the empty streets at prayer time – streets that are represented as beleaguered because of the excessive presence–absence of the Muslim resident. Likewise, the masculine yobbery exhibited by the Gallagher boys adds to the fears that unmanaged and intense proximity of the wrong kind can fuel violent animosity. Whether in separation or in closeness, the Gallagher kids' answers to inter-ethnic propinquity are pathologized and delegitimized within the national fantasy of multicultural intimacy, as uneducated, unruly, haphazard, and in need of appropriate patriarchal guidance. The problem with the Gallagher children is that they haven't domesticated their love or hate for another culture. More broadly, government strategies to redress the negative effects of inter-ethnic propinquity are decidedly located within working-class areas, which are the primary targets of corrective measures for instigating community cohesion and good neighbourliness. In this sense, the politics of mixing are about preventing working-class excesses and failures – in love, loathing, and indifference – and instilling British civil neighbourliness. Within this context, we can wonder about the extent to which the political repositioning of ethnic minorities in the public sphere, either as angry, rioting, or self-segregating guests, or as meritorious citizens who 'care back', is informed by a wider reconfiguration of classificatory schemes within the national collective that distinguish between two species: the 'neighbour from hell' and the 'heavenly neighbour'.

5 How does it feel? Feeling states and the limits of the civil nation

The ethos of this country is completely different from thirty years ago ... Offensive remarks and stupid stereotypes have been driven out of public conversation. The basic courtesies, in other words, have been extended to all people.

(Tony Blair 2006)

[C]ivility works through that elusiveness of desire and power[.]
(Roy 2005: 181)

Examining the ways that nations are imagined as *spaces of multicultural intimacy* points to considerations of a politics of inter-ethnic propinquity, where concerns of governance include the management, circulation, and dispersal of the 'ethnic' – in its racialized, religious, sexualized, gendered, classed, and generational inflections – within and across spatial and institutional units (such as the neighbourhood or the school). But it is more than that: it broadens the discussion in favour of an understanding of multiculturalist politics as intimately implicated with the management and circulation of *feelings for*, and *within*, the nation. The fantasy of multi-cultural intimacy is sustained through politics of inter-ethnic propinquity that are about physical relations in geographically bounded areas, as well as about the conception of non-physical relationships in terms of a spatial social imaginary; relationships that are imagined in the ambivalent spatial terms of obligations to and dangers of proximity. Multicultural intimacies are points of entanglement that are not only inscribed in a series of inclusions and exclusions – where excess is merely that which is left out – but they are also etched in the *desire* for the other while keeping him/her at a 'proper distance' (Sharma 2006: 106). This concluding chapter further excavates this double process of *rapprochement* and distancing, of embracing and repelling. In a series of six vignettes, I explore a range of feeling states that policy or popular representations and conceptions both produce and occlude by setting the discursive field within which the interactions depicted in each vignette take place. The previous chapters examined how various forms of multicultural intimacy are imagined in contemporary

Britain, and how the register of intimacy conjures up (national, local, individual) *bodies that feel*. One conclusion stemming from these chapters is that if the multicultural is universalized, deterritorialized, and disembodied as a *value*, it is also conceived as deeply localized and embodied as an *encounter*. Moreover, the *value* of the multicultural varies according to the *degree* and *kind* of proximities imagined between different cultures, as well as by the kinds of feelings it is said to ignite. Whether it is through the ingurgitation of flavours or hearing the 'bad English' spoken by waiters or waitresses,[1] whether it is through public displays of national pride, of the iconic 'multicultural child' as evidence of successful or failed 'integration', or of working-class excessive love, loathing, or indifference, *the encounter with multiculture is always conceived as a felt experience* and some of those experiences are marked as 'problems' of governance or as issues of public concern, while others are not. What kinds of encounters escape the government or public radar of concern, and which ones don't? Which kinds of intimacies are allowed to endure and in the name of what?

In this concluding chapter, I turn more squarely towards felt encounters, bodily and emotive, that are animated and mediated through ideals of multicultural intimacy that circulate in the public domain. The focus is on interactions *between* bodies and on the circulation and distribution of feelings between them as effecting, and as effects of, particular kinds of relations and intimacies – some distancing, some communing – that are in dialogue with wider cultural formations that inform the national structure of feeling. As Ahmed would argue, feelings are always mediated by how we understand the world around us,

> however immediately they seem to impress upon us. Not only do we read such feelings, but how the feelings feel in the first place [and what we 'do' with them] may be tied to a past history of readings, in the sense that the process of *recognition* (of this feeling, or that feeling) is bound up with what we *already know*.
>
> (Ahmed 2004: 25; emphasis original)

Thus, feeling states are not confined to the individual, indeed do not stop at the embodied self, but are constitutive of and constituted by national structures of feelings.[2] In short, the feeling body is also a thinking body, or a body that 'knows', a 'mindful body' as Elspeth Probyn puts it (drawing on Marcel Mauss's understanding of the habitus), which is consciously or unconsciously in 'dialogue with social structure' (Probyn 2005: 56) in a process of mutual ex/change. Thus the materials engaged in previous chapters are constitutive of a field of knowledge about multiculturalism; they are part of a multicultural horizon that is founded in, constitutive of, and prescriptive of how 'others' are regarded as threats or antagonists, or as friends and allies; of how 'others' are seen, perceived, pictured, imagined, and spoken of. In this sense, the concept of 'multicultural intimacy' fore-grounds the entanglement of technologies of reassurance with technologies of enmity. Far from condoning all forms of closeness, multicultural inti-macy is framed within a tight policing of community and family relations, consensual reproduction, and the choice of appropriate partners (friends, neighbours, or lovers). Central to the promotion of multicultural intimacy is what Elizabeth Povinelli calls the 'passions of recognition', where the collective mutual embrace remains 'inflected by the conditional' (2002: 17) – as long as racially or ethnically minoritized citizens adopt the nation and are available for adoption by the nation; as long as citizens are not repugnant; as long as they mix well. Who is intimate with whom, how, and under what circumstances, is not left to chance.

This is a key lesson we could draw from Ann Laura Stoler's work on the 'engineering of sentiment' in colonial regimes. Her fascinating account of the 'choreography of the everyday' in the Dutch Indies and French Indo-china – '[p]rescriptions for bathing, breastfeeding, cooking and sleeping arrangements' (Stoler 2002: 17) – excavates the microphysics of govern-ance in the management of sexual arrangement and affective attachment. Stoler insists on the racial codings of the politics of intimacy, and on the fundamental intertwining of the history of sexuality with the history of race, and argues that '[prescribed] sentiment as well as biology was what race was about' (Stoler 2002: 17). Likewise, I argue that the prescription of sentiment – of feelings for the nation, for the community, for the neigh-bour, for the Muslim, for the suicide-bomber, for minorities – is also what race and ethnicity are about. That is, the very act of naming who and how to love, suspect, befriend, care for, embrace, welcome, and so on, perfor-matively constructs racial, ethnic, cultural and national differences along with their gender, sexual, class, and generational 'identities'. Love, suspi-cion, fear, tolerance, pride, become markers of what multicultural intimacy is about; they are constitutive of various public feelings about the obliga-tions to and dangers of intimacy.

Stoler's work further reveals the effort that was put into separating individuals' visceral, bodily, and sensual feelings from emotional feelings; for example in ensuring that Dutch or French children growing up in the colonies did not 'feel at home' in those places, despite their immediate and intense felt encounters with 'natives' (e.g. nannies or wet nurses) or with the land and the surroundings. Much effort was put into separating 'the "feeling" of the world through the senses from the "feelings" that arise from those encounters' (Sheller 2004: 226). Following a Foucauldian vein, Stoler highlights how the *orientations* of sensations and cognitions *into* feelings are objects of technologies of governance. In other words, pre-scribed sentiments are attempts to orient desires and bodily sensations – how does it feel – into proper feelings – how do you feel. For the purposes of my argument here, this distinction usefully structures the distribution of the six vignettes.

Each vignette is to be read as part of a collage rather than a segment of an organized sequence that composes a neat linear plot. With this series of vignettes, I explore the ways in which various feelings fluctuate, operate, and are mobilized through elusive entanglements of desire and power (Roy 2005: 181) that are constitutive of the fantasy of multicultural intimacy. In other words, the vignettes capture different feeling states and their respective processes of dis/location; that is to say that the movement of feelings works differently on different bodies, and the encounters described below reveal how emotive and physical feelings themselves are sites of cultural exchange where history, politics, and social meaning are interwoven. More specifically, the vignettes aim to reveal various operations of power and subject production by depicting instances where the limits of civility come to bear. For example, what kinds of 'basic courtesies' (to cite Blair from the first epigraph) are required of and between inhabitants in multicultural Britain, on what grounds, and what are the limits? How is such an ostensibly innocuous gesture related to wider operations of power, governance, and subject production?

How does it feel?

Vignette 1: sensescapes

Attempts to include or exclude minorities hinge on perceptions of habits or preferences, which are taken up as signifiers of entire 'lifestyles' and which are encountered through different sensory fields: the smell of the neighbour's cooking wafting through your net curtains; or the sound of the banghra, hip-hop or rock beats pounding out of the car at the stop light; or the sight of the group of hoodies hanging around in the market square. Some encounters are welcome, some are not, but all are deeply felt and confront subjects with the limits of their own boundaries. For example, when the sound of wailing in hospices disrupts the 'usual' (i.e. white British) way of grieving and moves carers to negotiate their positions as professionals in their attempts to deal with the 'disruptive' grief and the grievances of those complaining about it, as Yasmin Gunaratnam evocatively captures (2006). Or when the 'lively' sound of different languages spoken at the newsagent, when seasonal migrant workers are around, becomes a 'barrier' when the migrants turn into 'asylum-seekers' held in the local asylum centre (Willcox 2002).[3] Or finally, when two 'suspicious looking' 'Middle Eastern looking men', allegedly 'speaking Arabic' (which turns out to be Urdu), board a plane bound to Manchester from Malaga causes other passengers to tense up and to sharpen their gaze into a scrutinizing stare. And when the passengers' fears becomes such that the men are evicted from the plane and put through another security check, only to be allowed on board another flight so they could return home – to Manchester.[4]

At those moments, embodied and emotive feelings materialize, and are materialized through, boundaries of belonging and of 'community'. Gail Lewis uses an evocative phrase – 'practices of skin' (2004b: 122 *inter alia*) – to speak of those actions that give meaning to certain kinds of interactions and experience through the making of racial categories. 'Practices of skin' include practices of *marking* – how staring at the men *makes* them 'Middle Eastern' and suspect (and male) and *makes* other passengers threatened and *entitled* to be afraid (and white). At the same time, such practices of skin also re-form 'that social space through re-forming the apartness' (Ahmed 2004: 54) of the different bodies. This is an apartness that is not only about visible or audible differences issuing from the body, but is an 'apartness' that is also founded on the circulation and distribution of emotive feelings across and between bodies. As Divya Tolia-Kelly puts it, '[a] body that is signified as a source of fear through its markedness cannot be free to affect and be affected similarly to the one that is not' (2006: 215).

Vignette 2: not feeling

The fantasy of multicultural intimacy incorporates a twofold desire to feel and to not feel ethno-racial-cultural-national borders,[5] insofar as it is framed within commodity multiculturalism, where multiculture is a mode of acquiring a 'taste' for difference. This is what Ghassan Hage refers to as cosmo-multiculturalism which he describes as a:

> mode of consuming *diversity* [which] can only be done by maintaining a certain distance from the materiality of the [production of the] food consumed so that the experience is not just that of eating a hot curry that causes sweat, but to 'eat' [and *feel*] that very difference between the curry and the pesto.
>
> (1997: 128–9; second emphasis added)

One of the logics of cosmo-multiculturalism is the logic of appreciation, or distinction, between the classy cosmopolitan person who has accumulated 'cosmopolitan capital' (Hage 1997: 137) and the unclassy person who hasn't or who refuses to cross and feel that border. Here, racial and class privilege is performed not in terms of unfettered mobility across borders – as the familiar trope of globalization goes – but rather through the desire to *feel* the 'border' of cultural difference in a pleasurable way.

The class dynamics structuring the fantasy of multicultural intimacy were tellingly manifest in two separate televised visits to Brick Lane, East London.[6] The first was by author, political commentator, and radio talk-show host Andrew Marr (2000a, 2000b). The second, by Matthew Taylor (2001), then director of the Institute for Public Policy Research, an independent think tank generally perceived as left leaning.[7] Taylor visited Brick Lane with local resident Terry Penton, who we see watching disdainfully as

Taylor tastes the different fare on offer and delightfully tells the camera that 'multiculturalism is very very fattening'. Marr, for his part, wanders the streets of Brick Lane marvelling at its available diversity, and remarks that:

> within a few hundred yards, you can journey from the old East End, with jellied eel and whelk stalls, elderly men in 1950s-style suits, junk shops stacked with old shellac records and moist, moulded furniture, to the London of the 2000s, with coldly trendy clothes shops, cutting-edge new Asian restaurants, impossibly fashionable cafés, and walls covered with Indian film posters. On busy days, the air is full of Bangladeshis, American, French and Asian voices. The massive old Truman Brewery has been bought by an Iraqi who is turning it into a set of new media, film PR, design and arts spaces, the cutting-edge businesses of modern London.
>
> (2000a: 158)

For Marr, the culture produced by the new-wave Asians and Iraqis provides the path to the future of multi-ethnic Britain. The future is here, *not* in the working class 'old East End'. For both men, the problem of multi-cultural Britain is turned into the problem of abject, bland, musty, and retrograde, working-class Britain whose refusal to feel is condemned as a refusal to engage with, meet, and welcome, the other. Not feeling the borders across cultures is thus, at times, presented as a failure to 'do' multi-cultural intimacy. Like the white working-class in London's East End, the 'self-segregating' ethnic communities of North England are also admonished for not doing multiculture. Furthermore, as shown in Chapter 4, concerns about the nature and intensity of inter-ethnic propinquity decidedly target working-class areas. Thus the fantasy of multicultural intimacy is about preventing working-class failures, but also about preventing excesses of feeling – of not wanting to feel (such as genial indifference), but also in feeling too much (be it in love or loathing).

At another level, however, not feeling is an integral part of the world that the fantasy of multicultural intimacy conjures up insofar as it seeks to *transcend* differences within the diluted 'rich mix' that makes 'us' what we are today (Blair 2000). Overall, while migrants and ethnic minorities are welcome for their contribution to the British economic growth and to the consumerist landscape, there is also, as David Parker argues, a 'disavowal of their distinctive social and political claims' (2000: 78; also Hutnyk 2000). Ghassan Hage's 'cosmo-multiculturalism' captures how the celebration and consumption of diversity exists alongside the devaluation of the physical presence of migrants: this is a 'multiculturalism without migrants' (1997: 118). The circulation of 'ethnicity' as a 'taste' – gustative, visual, aesthetic – celebrates and consumes diversity alongside the devaluation of the physical and political presence of migrants. New Labour is much more concerned with individuals respecting diversity as a *value*, than it is with considering the material and political conditions of its production, circulation, and consumption. The multicultural spectacle of national diversity is a mutation of 'the long Western colonialist tradition of exhibiting the national self through the exhibiting of otherness' (Hage in Gunew 2004: 29). Here, the national self is not confirmed in its opposition to an external other, but rather, the exhibitions of national diversity mirror the collective self as rich with diversity and serve to shore up national hegemony and national self-love in the continual replay of motifs that seek to *rewrite the national same so that 'we' could love ourselves as different*. This motif is what *Multicultural Horizons* unravels.

Thus the national comfort with diversity is produced through the displacement of difference in favour of a more palatable diversity that ignores the social and political claims of minoritized subjects and that refuses to name the difference, so that I/'we' don't have to feel or recognize it, or indeed think about it. This 'ludic multiculturalism' (Matuštík 1998) depoliticizes culture, aestheticizes politics, and commodifies ethnicity. The migrant-as-ethnic is invited *on*, not *at*, the kitchen table. At the same time, 'culture' is re-injected into debates over the presence and dispersal of migrants within the nation and its impact on the demographics and sociality of local communities (Chapter 4) or of educational, care, and welfare institutions. In such contexts, for those whose bodies are marked as different, the crossing borders or thresholds in the intercultural interactions that the everydayness of multiculture is made of comes with their bodies being 'travelled upon' (Puar 1994). Marked and read as threatening, dubious, ambiguous, immoral, inferior, undesirable other, 'some bodies must always negotiate the discursive structures that render [them] Other' (Puar 1994: 93) and consequently must *always* feel the border.

Vignette 3: 'I feel good in my skin'

When asked why they chose to stay in Montreal, many white Anglo-Canadian migrants to Quebec would tell me that it is because in Montreal, *je suis bien dans ma peau* – 'I feel good in my skin'. This phrase explicitly suggests how migration is lived through practices of skin, yet begs the question about the 'sensory regimes' (Thomas 2004; also Wise and Chapman 2005) and economies of feeling that structure migration and border crossing. To suggest *je suis bien dans ma peau* is to imply that I can sink into my skin because I am comfortable, at ease with the environment. For Ahmed (2004: 148), 'sinking in' is about fitting into an environment and my body disappearing from view. But isn't this very expression returning us to our body, to a time and a place when perhaps one wasn't comfortable, or to the realization that I thought I was comfortable, but that in fact I wasn't as comfortable as I thought I was. To declare *je suis bien dans ma peau* returns me to my body and to a place from my past, before I can carry on moving and living comfortably in the streets of the city and perhaps disappearing into it.

Crucially, this statement asks the question of the kinds of social spaces and interactions Montreal is made of that can afford some people to sink into their skin and disappear from view. Is such a comfort available to all, at all times? I certainly stopped feeling *bien dans ma peau* after being sexually harassed and threatened by two men as I was on my favourite walk on the Mont Royal; or when I could no longer endure the sustained and insistent menacing stare of hate that a nearby man cast on me and my girlfriend as we were sitting on a park bench one warm summer day, and I enjoined her to leave for a safer space.

My friend Aisha also didn't feel *bien dans sa peau* when asked the cliché question: 'where are your from? ... No [pause] where are you *really* from?' Does the woman wearing a hijab or a niqab feel *bien dans sa peau* after being attacked and taunted in the high street, or fired from her teaching job? When *does* one feel good in her skin and how does it relate to encounters that bring her back to her body and skin with a vengeance? How does feeling good in one's skin relate to how encounters – lived or imagined – reshape the apartness of bodies from other bodies and from the social location that they are moving through and inhabiting?

The examples above illustrate how the privileges of invisibility, of one's body disappearing from view, can be fragile and contingent. Moreover, such privileges are themselves performed, reinstated, or withdrawn through bodily interactions and performances of 'civil inattention' and 'uncivil attention'. Carol Gardner inverted Ervin Goffman's notion of civil inattention, that is:

> the ways we feign indifference in public life so as to grant recognition to those around us but to deem that they are of no threat. Uncivil attention involved forms of public harassment – abuse, harryings and annoyances – that exist on a continuum of possible actions, ending with violence.
>
> (Gardner in Noble 2005: 112)

For many minoritized subjects, feigned indifference is sometimes a welcome respite from the kind of uncivil attention that moves on a continuum from the simply annoying to the utterly terrifying. It is worth specifying that uncivil attention is not only about aggression. It can also include the kinds of curiosity and intimate questions about one's 'way of life' that comes with being the 'exotic' or unwanted other in the room: from 'why do you wear a veil?' to the loud and public question 'is this the women's WC?' when a butch walks into a public washroom, or the curious yet embarrassed stares at a disabled person getting on a bus. In these instances the minoritized bodies are always put in their place and reminded of their minority status, while their personal boundaries are made permeable and penetrable, shrunk back to the geography closest in, to their skin and body and inner feelings, as the majoritized subject gets closer and more personal. What remains invisible in the courteous world of multicultural tolerance are the numerous *discourtesies* that minoritized individuals are subjected to at the institutional as well as at the informal levels of daily life. What remains invisible in the courteous world of multicultural intimacy is any understanding of the pressures of minoritized subjects to perform the required civil attention to the nation – graciously answering the intrusive questions, bowing to the insistent stare, or removing the niqab – while they are subjected to persistent uncivil attention. The infamous veil row triggered by Jack Straw is an example.

How do you feel?

Vignette 4: failed/failing feeling

Women wearing the niqab make Jack Straw, Tony Blair, and many others, Muslims and non-Muslims, uncomfortable. In October 2006, the then Leader of the House of Commons Jack Straw wrote about a meeting with a constituent in his office in Blackburn (northern England). Though it was probably not his first encounter with a Muslim woman wearing the face veil known as the 'niqab', Straw seems to have felt it was time to publicly express his feelings of discomfort. In a blog run by the *Lancashire Telegraph*, he wrote: 'I felt uncomfortable about talking to someone "face-to-face" who I could not see' (Straw 2006). The 'full veil' [sic], according to Straw, makes 'better, positive relations between the two communities more difficult' (Straw 2006). Though several Labour MPs distanced themselves from Straw's position and public opinion about his remark was very mixed, Tony Blair, as well as several commentators and editorials, supported Straw for speaking out on what was regarded as a threat to good community relations. Tony Blair's view was that the niqab worn by some Muslim women is 'a mark of separation and that is why it makes other people from outside of the community feel uncomfortable' (in Woodward 2006). The *Guardian* reported that when '[a]sked if it was possible for a woman wearing a veil to make a full contribution to British society, Mr Blair said it was "a very difficult question"' (Woodward 2006).[8] Though Blair refused to go down the line of dictating to Muslim women what not to wear (as in France, Italy, Belgium, the Netherlands, some states in Germany, or Quebec), his refusal to give a straight answer about veiled women making a contribution to society is telling of the limits of British tolerance and recognition. As Douglas Crimp wrote, 'tolerance is, as Pasolini said, "always and purely nominal," merely "a more refined form of condemnation"' (1989: 11). In the 'veil row' of autumn 2006, women who conceal their faces under the niqab stood accused of enforcing separation rather than integration. Muslim women – and Muslims more generally – were cast as thieves of the national comfort.

The assumption is that what you wear is an expression of an entire culture, identity, and identification *against* the British national. In Chapter 3, I suggest that the hijab is normalized, banalized, made benign as it is cast against other forms of dress deemed more abject and suspect. The 'veil row', in this regard, is part of an ongoing process of organization and systemitization of a disciplining gaze that constructs distinctions between the moderate and the fanatic, and between citizens who are willing and those who are unwilling to reassure fellow nationals. In early 2005, a 16-year-old schoolgirl, Shabina Begum, took her high school to court in a fight for the right to wear the jilbab at school (after two appeals by the school, she eventually lost her case at the Judicial Committee of the House of Lords). In numerous newspaper accounts of this case, the public was taught to associate the jilbab with a degree of Muslim orthodoxy that made the jilbab undesirable and indeed threatening. One particular account in the *Telegraph* (Petre 2005) offered a short overview of the different styles of dress which were placed on a continuum from the more moderate to the strictest: the hijab, the shalwar kameeze, the jilbab, the burkha. It is not the information as such that I was disturbed by, but the context and manner in which it was dispensed. The *Telegraph*'s didacticism educated the public into a disciplining gaze through which it can distinguish between acceptable and threatening Muslims. Readers were taught to recognize the moderate and to seek the fundamentalist, as their gaze was directed at Muslim women's bodies that onlookers are invited to pay 'uncivil attention' to, to linger on, to decipher, to dismember, and to read for signs of religious orthodoxy. Looking back at Muslim EMMA in Chapter 3 in the light of this wider context, she represents a particular version of Muslim Britain and suggests the limits of toleration that works through the aesthetic disciplining and normalization of the population as a whole: the good model of Muslim Britain as moderately traditional and modern, and the non-Muslim onlooker who can tell the difference. Moreover, school authorities and some of Begum's peers were quoted as saying that their opposition to her request was based on the fear that it would attract radical Muslims to the school and that they would seek to indoctrinate vulnerable young women. In the arguments supporting the school's decision to refuse Begum, the onus was put on Begum to protect the school against the possibility of unwanted Islamic intrusion, and she was reprimanded for failing to reassure her peers. The various 'veil rows', then, are instances where, as Greg Noble writes, '[o]ur comfortable and relaxed nation ... rests increasingly on the discomfort of strangers' (2005: 119), that is, on them understanding *themselves* as 'nuisances' (Sayad in Noble 2005: 111), consequently being called upon to reassure the nation and restore its comfort by redressing their behaviour.

At the same time, we are taught that the variations of degrees should not distract us from the fact that these vestments are signs of a sex/gender system that is, even in its moderate manifestation, 'less equal' to the British one and that it is an expression of inherent cultural differences. Jack Straw (2006) expressed his 'surprise' when '[i]t became absolutely clear to [him] that the husband had played no part in her [his constituent's] decision' to wear the niqab. Several of Shabina Begum's detractors stated that she was coerced into wearing the jilbab by her brother Shuweb Rahman, allegedly a supporter of the radical Islamist group Hizb ut-Tahrir, who had allegedly assumed undue authority over her following their parents' death. Muslim women's attire 'invites an aggressive heterosexual patriotism' (Puar and Rai 2002: 117), that is, a policing of their behaviour in the name of a putative feminism that prescribes the kinds of femininity and domestic life that fit within the national fantasy of romantic love, marriage, and familial arrangements. Such prescriptions are concealed within the fantasy of the liberal, civil society ostensibly ruled by states and legal systems, not by culture, and that protects the fiction of the sovereign subject under the cloak of choice which 'blinds us to powers producing that subject' (Brown 2006: 197). The unease caused by the women wearing the niqab is that they are claiming a 'difference' *in their own terms*, and that several are doing so voluntarily. This scuppers the culturalist view underpinning British multicultural horizons that assumes that 'culture' collides with feminism and that Muslim women cannot think for themselves. Thus when women 'surprise' men like Straw with their choices, the fundaments of 'difference' unravel.

These fundaments are grounded in a dualistic framework of 'traditional' and 'modern' which is often juxtaposed over 'past' and 'present'. For Blair, the veil brings up an important debate about the degree of 'integration' of Muslims in Britain and about 'how Islam comes to terms with and is comfortable with the modern world' (in Woodward 2006). Similarly, the former Home Office Secretary David Blunkett aligned himself with the late Pym Fortuyn,[9] who Blunkett says 'had a point about the clash of modernity with long held cultural traditions' because:

[there is a] continuing tension between modernity and the cultural practices of some of those entering highly-advanced countries. This is not true, of course, for the majority of those entering the more developed world, but it is for those who, because of education or geography, find themselves catapulted into effectively different centuries. *They are making a journey in the space of a few weeks or months, which has taken us hundreds of years to make.* Recognising and helping people with this change is as much part of the job of the settled community of similar religion and culture as it is of the host nation, and this is one of the challenges that we need to face. Accepted norms *hundreds of years ago in this country*, but *now rejected*, remain acceptable from particular cultures of varying religions.

(Blunkett 2002: 68; emphasis added)

The temporal and the spatial merge within a distinction between a 'more developed' *here* and a 'less developed' or 'developing' *there*, producing what

Anne McClintock refers to as 'anachronistic space' where '[g]eographical differences across *space* is figured as historical difference across *time*' (McClintock 1995: 40; emphasis original). Britain's imaginative geography remains primarily conceived in culturalist terms that separate the good from the bad, the civilized from the barbaric, where the latter is not only outside, but also within the nation. Within this framework, concerns about 'integration' are about securing the fantasy of a modern a-cultural, united, and coherent national whole against its internal cultural dangers, thus legitimating actions of uncivil attention in the name of protecting the national comfort.

Finally, it is noteworthy that the veil row, which emphasizes a visible difference that hinders the capacity to see, came in the aftermath of the unease caused by the 'enemy within' who escapes visibility. As argued in Chapter 3, the 'unremarkableness' of the suicide bombers of 7/7, and of the suspected ones of August 2006, became a mantra-like reiteration of their uncanny invisibility and forced (yet again) the realization of the limits of a regime of looking that combined skin colour with cultural markers – the veil, the beard, the tunic – in order to shore up and secure the investment in the symbolic position of 'Whiteness' as the ideal of Britishness (c.f. Seshadri-Crooks 2000). With the veil row, the tensions and contradictions around in/visibility come to light: the tensions that oppose the unease about the enemy who escapes the visibility of cultural markers, on the one hand, and the unease about the neighbour who is too visible, on the other. The shifting structure of visibility and invisibility becomes the source of discomfort that troubles the national fantasy of multicultural intimacy, as the physical appearance and clothes of these minoritized subjects mark them 'as both original and derivative' (Roy: 2005: 181). This ambivalence of the 'Other' bothers the nation/al, because his/her desires seem indecipherable, split between 'there' (the original) and 'here' (the derivative), and unclearly directed – are they here or there? Where and how does *this* nation/al fit in the Other's desires? Consequently, as Roy argues, '[t]his disruptive permeability between the "inner" and the "outer" makes the [minoritized 'ethnic' subject] the object of continual scrutiny' (2005: 181). In multicultural Britain, this ambivalence is worked out in attempts to restore the stable gaze of the national subject through various technologies of reassurance seen to orient and contain ethnic subjects' feelings into feelings for the nation.

Vignette 5: How do you feel ... at heart?

Since the attacks on London's transport system in July 2005, the revived discussions in the Home Office and in the public domain about seeking new ways to 'celebrate Britishness' all indicate the attention, concern, and in some instances effort that goes into the 'internal states' of *some* citizens – how do you/they feel, *at heart* – and not simply on their display of educational credentials, or cultural competence in Britishness and 'life in the United Kingdom'.[10] Suggestions have ranged from former Home Office Minister Paul Goggins's 'citizenship ceremonies for every 18 year old regardless of background or birthplace' (Hinsliff *et al.* 2005), to former Home Office Minister of State Hazel Blears's suggestion to 're-brand' ethnic minorities with hyphenated identities, or former Tory Leader Michael Howard's call for fostering a stronger understanding of Britishness amongst ethnic minorities (Howard 2005), and former Chancellor of the Exchequer Gordon Brown's plea for the 'new urgency' of inculcating pride and patriotism in the British population (G. Brown 2006). This emotivist agenda is underpinned by the assumption that feelings such as anger or national disloyalty are integral to an entire culture, which in turn carries the elements for a *possible* radicalism. The assumption is that one's 'culture' is the problem and replacing it with a strong sense of national belonging will be the solution – as illustrated in Will Hutton's commentary discussed in Chapter 3. Since July 2005, then, a shift of emphasis has occurred within discourses of integration, towards patriotism, solidarity, and 'community of feeling'. In contrast to the diagnosis following inquests into the causes of the 2001 riots where 'mixing' was prescribed as an antidote to racism and segregation, the concerns this time focus on the need to instil Britishness in the *heart* of all minorities, suggesting that however 'ordinary' their lives may appear, they are always already suspect of being 'not-us *at heart*' (cf. Povinelli 2002: 17; emphasis added). This is not to say that such suspicions are new – the conflation, in Britain, of 'immigrant' with 'black' and/or 'foreigner' predates present day Britain and has always implied that some 'others' are not British, at heart. However, the terms of inclusion and the articulation of what constitutes the national 'we' have shifted into a new arrangement and different emphasis – the emphasis on values and its impact on different degrees of differences attributed to different groups, as discussed in Chapter 1 – while the focus remains the same – ethnic minorities and the maintenance of white British hegemony, the form of which is changing in relation to the particular historical conditions that impact on its definition. Hence, since 9/11 and revived apace in the immediate aftermath of 7/7, Muslims in Britain are repeatedly pressed to disavow their connection with Muslim radicals and to state their allegiance to Britain. Les Back *et al.* have noted a shift between October 2000 and post-2001, in the terms of inclusion offered to ethnic minorities, from the outright injunction to be a proud Briton to an 'injunction to be moderate' (2002: 3.13). We can now note the deep intertwining of both. To be a proud Briton – and to be a Briton that makes the nation proud, as seen in Chapter 2 – *is* to be moderate. The clichéd question in the well-known scenario of misrecognition that goes: 'Where are you from? No. (Pause) Where are you *really* from?' now comes with 'And how do you feel about this nation? No. (Pause) How do you *really* feel?'

Vignette 6: feelings of re/assurance

A guiding principle of the Blair government was that a strong sense of individual and self identity must be the necessary condition for community cohesion: a 'feel good' politics premised on dialogue, faith and mutual understanding (see Chapter 4). The premise is, in the words of David Blunkett's foreword to the White Paper on nationality, immigration, and asylum, '[t]o enable integration to take place, and to value the diversity it brings, *we need to be secure in our sense of belonging and identity* and therefore to be able to reach out and to embrace those who come to the UK' (Blunkett 2001: 1; emphasis added). For Blunkett, love thyself comes first, and then comes loving thy neighbour. Hence, several technologies of citizenship have been sought, proposed, or put in place as means of securing the national white Britons' sense of, and entitlement to, Britishness – indeed much of the government's reassessment of the value of multiculturalism revolves around the comfort of 'white Britons', as Ruth Kelly clearly stated (2006). Some of these technologies are deployed in spectacles of national communities of feeling. Mabel Berezin writes of national communities of feeling as generating 'emotional energy in support or against the polity' (2002: 39). Her interest is in *when* emotions are transposed into some sort of action or institutional arrangement; when do we or don't we act emotionally. Though I do not approach emotions as she does – as something that can be turned on or off – I do take her point about the belief of political elites in the potential emotional energy of political spectacle. In Britain, New Labour ministers, past and present, such as David Blunkett and Gordon Brown, have expressed their belief in the potential of ceremonies and symbols in fostering feelings for the nation. The hope is that symbolic events will redress or contain identitarian practices *within* the national domestic space, thus reassuring 'the nation' of its strength and coherence through the public spectacle of feelings for the nation. Consider for example the new citizenship ceremony, initially recommended by the Cantle Report (Home Office 2001a) – the first of which occurred on 26 February 2004 – and conceived as the crowning moment of a training programme in English language and citizenship. Culminating in swearing an oath to the Queen, reciting the 'citizenship pledge' to uphold British democratic values, and singing the national anthem, the ceremonies are meant to ritualistically and symbolically seal the social contract newcomers are committing themselves to when taking on British citizenship. At the same time, the ceremonies perpetuate the idea that newcomers have to publicly display their commitment to their new country of residence, thus reassuring the nation of their allegiance. As David Blunkett stated on the occasion of the first ceremony, citizenship ceremonies

> will be the answer to those who fear difference, who fear the diversity which comes with people coming across the world to live in our community

and sends a clear message that those who choose to be part of the [British] family are committing themselves.

(Johnston 2004; Morris and Akbar 2004).

The ceremony is both an individualizing and collectivizing device, invested as it is with the belief in the significance of rituals, not only in fostering individual feelings for the nation, but in reassuring the nation's long-standing citizens of newcomers' propriety and legitimacy. Being 'secure in our sense of belonging and identity' for Blunkett, is not for *all* inhabitants of Britain. Rather, it is specifically about reassuring established nationals rather than challenging existing racisms and discriminatory practices and institutions. Citizenship ceremonies are a fitting example of the entanglement of technologies of reassurance with technologies of enmity within the fantasy of national unity, as they demarcate a distinction between the good established citizens who need reassuring, the new citizens who need confirmation of their propriety, and the failed citizens – those who do not 'choose to be part of the family' or who fail to 'act British'. Within this entangled web of entitlement and belonging, some citizens are always already suspect and full citizenship will never be fully achieved.

In addition, the ceremonies are also an occasion where the nation can indulge in its own vanity and further instantiate its love for itself. 'Being British is something of a blessing and a privilege for us all', stated Prince Charles at the first ceremony (in Johnston 2004), and the *Sunday Express* proudly stated that 'we can rightly celebrate our tolerance' (Callan 2004). With the words of new citizens widely cited – words of happiness, relief, and gratitude – the nation can be reminded of its tolerance and goodness, and, in some sections of the press, of its hopes for newcomers' contributions to the betterment of national life.

The limits of the civil nation

The citizenship ceremonies are an apposite place to conclude. Combining spectacle, ritual, and governance, the ceremonies are sites where citizenship is ceremoniously bestowed in an atmosphere of high emotional intensity: people cry, are elated, or simply relieved, but all participate in a public performance of national allegiance that reasserts the uniqueness of the nation they are joining. Citizenship ceremonies are not the place to declare any ardent attachment to a particular culture or religion, or to anything of any other sort – even patriotism is to be moderate if it is to be acceptable. Rather, it is the place to promise one's allegiance and loyalty to more abstract state institutions and to the rules of democracy. The ceremonies are a good example of how the fantasy of multicultural intimacy is a protective fiction that, haunted by its potential failure to stabilize desirable forms of attachment, seeks to create and sustain the myth of the 'national family' and its promise of fullness, coherence, and solidarity. The fantasy of multicultural intimacy is integral to the emergence of a British national formation of toleration that is founded on the proclamation of the equal worth of all cultures while declaring the need for overriding national values. These values set the limits of multicultural intimacy, and produce, as Elizabeth Povinelli (2002: 27) argues, a 'civil nation' from these limits by referring to 'universal' moral values – pride, good neighbourliness, romantic love, moderate religious faith, tolerance, solidarity – that some practices violate – dissent, genial indifference, working-class male street violence, diasporic belongings, 'queer' familial arrangements, or un-moderate religious practice and devotion.

The forms of sociality prescribed in ideals of mixing, loving thy neighbour, national pride, tolerance, and extending the 'basic courtesies' to all citizens call for some kind of 'emotional labor' (Hochschild 1983) in the work of transmuting and managing personal feelings into public acts that are recognizable within the realm of civility. The feeling states of multiculturalism are organized around an *economy* of feelings: the production, circulation, and distribution of legitimate feelings for and within the nation, where the burden of that labour largely falls upon those in minoritized positions – working-class, women, ethnic minorities, younger generations – who are often required to make the majoritized subject feel better. The vignettes above further highlight the currency of feelings and their differential value within the wider economic structure of feelings that delineates the codes of conduct of good multicultural citizenry. And their exchange value is political: different feelings are attributed different values – or rather, they are differentially located within the 'national values' against which the 'value' of citizens is assessed. As Jack Katz might put it, individuals face the dilemma of abandoning or joining the community, or being abandoned or embraced by the community, when 'loyalty to the [nation] is pitted against loyalty to the *values* that make the [nation] an honorable collectivity' (1999: 154; emphasis added). This was made explicit by Tony Blair when he told Muslims: 'Our tolerance is part of what makes Britain, Britain. So conform to it or don't come here' (2006).

In December 2006, Blair explicitly made tolerance not only a value, but a duty that, when fulfilled, grants individuals 'the *right* to be in a multicultural society' (emphasis added). Tolerance in Blair's injunction rightly addresses all forms of discriminatory practices – from white racism to fundamentalist Islam. However, in his speech, the radical and the moderate Muslim all merge into one, and the niqab-wearing 'ordinary' Muslim woman is aligned with the fundamentalist waging war on the Western world. That is where the limits of civil society pull at the seams: when the universalized values of the civil nation work through fixing a fundamentalist other. Tolerance operates not only through marking the minority as minority, but also as intolerant. The superiority and value of the universal is confirmed by the non-reciprocal response on the part of the particular who 'does not tolerate the universal' (W. Brown 2006: 186). Muslims appear as more thoroughly saturated by their religion and incapable of tolerating non-Muslim particularities, as seen in Chapter 4. Blair is implying that Muslims are not tolerant and are not abiding by the rule of law that requires them to tolerate and integrate with other faiths; the implication is that Muslims are ruled by an authoritarian religion and culture that will not integrate and that will threaten Britain's liberal, multicultural ethos of intimacy with tolerance.

Blair's 'basic courtesies' are performative insofar as they become the means by which to transcend differences – they are 'extended to all people' – and to promulgate the fiction that Britain is inherently tolerant and that it condemns intolerant, racist behaviours in public spaces. Indeed, 'basic courtesies' are performances of the nation/al *public* persona – its presentation of self. Hence, at one level, the issue is about the performance of self so that Britain *appears* intolerant of racism on the international scene. Thus, Blair cites the driving out of offensive remarks from public conversation as evidence that racism has 'been kicked out of sport' (2006), while he ignores how ethnic minorities are still largely under-represented in managerial and decision-making positions (Back *et al.* 2001; King 2004; Phillips n.d.). Or in response to a public outcry about racist abuse proffered on the television series *Celebrity Big Brother* against Indian Bollywood star Shilpa Shetty by at least two of her housemates, a spokesman for Tony Blair said that 'What clearly is to be regretted and countered is *any perception abroad* that in any way we tolerate racism in this country' (Gibson *et al.* 2007; emphasis added). The public performance of tolerance through silence protects the nation against embarrassment, conceals the less visible workings of institutional and other forms of racism, and reasserts British civility; a civility that has its historical roots in domestic and colonial economics of class and gender (Roy 2005; Markley 2006). Consider how Blair and most sections of the press did not question Channel 4's denial, at the beginning of the *Big Brother* controversy, that any racist abuse had taken place, stating that the term actually used against Shetty was 'cunt', not 'Paki'. In an extraordinary statement, Channel 4 explained that if the word had been 'Paki', it would not have bleeped it 'in order to highlight an aspect of his [contestant Jack Tweed's] character' (Holmwood and Brook 2007). So the limits of civility are clearly drawn here along gendered and racial lines – where sexist abuse is acceptable and simply censored as an offensive word, but not indicative of a noteworthy 'character trait' in a game show where competitors are judged on their character. At the same time, 'racism' is contained and privatized as an individual character trait that has no place in British civil society. The racist is quarantined, and the sexist is overlooked.

Readers will note that we have moved from citizenship ceremonies, to Blair's speech and *Celebrity Big Brother*; through various feeling states of everyday life; from pride politics, to children of multicultural Britain, to the politics of inter-ethnic propinquity; all these moves took us through

British multicultural horizons that are indicative of 'just how ordinary are the complexities – and anxieties – of "race" in the modern UK ... just how deep a part of the everyday "national" culture "race" really is' (Lewis 2004b: 112). Equally ordinary are anxieties about sex, gender, and kinship – anxieties that become sites of displacement for wider political fears about the national future. Race and kinship merge and co-emerge in the fantasy of the neo-liberal citizen, where feelings are de-culturalized and privatized. Britain's multicultural horizons are invested with a fantasy of multicultural intimacy that is not concerned with defining culture, but rather with the status of the state and its power to confer or withdraw recognition for forms of alliance – sexual, racial, cultural (Butler 2002: 22). As Butler suggests, 'the state becomes the means by which a [national] fantasy becomes literalized: desire[,] sexuality[, race] are ratified, justified, known, publicly instated, imagined as permanent, durable' (2002: 22). What the national fantasy conceals is how messy, slippery, and fragile 'racial' differences and kinship formations actually are, how porous cultural boundaries can be, how fluid cultural practices are, and how experiences of racialized or culturalized differences are uneven across class, gender, generational, and urban/regional divides (Lewis 2004b: 112).

Thinking critically about the limits of the civil nation, then, is not to position oneself as advocating uncivil, intolerant behaviour. Rather, a critical understanding of the limits of civility is to take seriously the claims of justice and equality invested in ideals of civility and to be alert to the articulations of inequality, abjection, subordination, and colonial violence that are suppressed in the fantasy of the 'civil nation' (W. Brown 2006: 205). It is to expose the material and historical conditions under which particular 'categories', 'identities', and identifications come about, circulate, and come to occupy a particular position in the national landscape. It is to attend to issues of category, power, and the locations of the organization/management of multiple identities and intercultural encounter. It is to challenge the anti-historical, depoliticizing aims of 'feel-good' multiculturalism, or the reductionist critiques of multiculturalism as merely culturalist and separatist, by rethinking conflict through grammars of power and struggle that recognize everyone's feeling states as historically constituted and by recognizing that we are *all* social and historical subjects. The politics of multiculture are not just about feelings, but feelings are an integral element of neo-liberal governing strategies, just as feelings are integral to justice, which multiculturalism, lest we forget, is also about.

Postscript

As I write these lines in April 2007, the Blair era is coming to a close (Blair is expected to resign in May 2007) and Gordon Brown, Blair's likely successor, is poised to take on the leadership of New Labour and to act as Prime Minister for an indeterminate period of time. On the Conservative side, David Cameron is shaking up the party with his neo-liberal agenda and emotivist ethos evocatively captured in his much derided 'hug a hoodie' call for more tolerance for minoritized subjects. As I write these lines, the future of multicultural Britain is uncertain, but looming on the horizon is the disappearance of multiculturalism from political and public debate. Both Brown and Cameron have spoken of multiculturalism in the past tense – Brown relegating it as a 'once-fashionable view' which 'over-emphasised separateness at the cost of unity' (2007) – and they share a vision of a post-multicultural British future that retrieves and aggrandizes past glories of Empire and of the Great British Union (it is worth noting that 2007 is also the year of the 300th anniversary of 1707 Act of Union, and the 200th anniversary of the abolition of the slave trade).

That *Multicultural Horizons* is critical of how multiculturalism relates to the operations of power does not make it a book against multiculturalism altogether. The disappearance of multiculturalism from public debate would be a sad state of affairs indeed, as it would leave even less room for critical discussion about the terms of multiculturalism, as this book offers, and less room for the recognition of the limits of the ideal of national wholeness. What worries me is the replacement of multiculturalism with a fiercer and more adamant assertion of the Nation Thing and of the possibility of full national representation, which clears a space for more, rather then less, inequality, resentment, and hostility against those whose 'cultural identity' and 'cultural ways' are marked as hindering national unity and disturbing national comfort. At least when multiculture is openly discussed, the nation/al confronts its own limits and there is still room for some creativity in thinking differently about living with difference. However, the disappearance of multiculturalism from public and political debates does not mean the disappearance of multicultural Britain. Therein lies my hope for the future: in the small lives of ordinary people who remind us of the productive gaps between state stipulation and normative discourses, and the politics of everyday social life.

Notes

1 Horizons of intimacies

1. Often referred to by the names of its co-chairmen, the 'Laurendeau-Dunton Commission' was appointed to examine existing bilingualism and biculturalism, and to recommend ways of ensuring wider recognition of the basic cultural dualism of Canada. Book Four of the Commission's report, CRCBB 1969, dealt with the contribution of ethnic minorities to the cultural enrichment of Canada, and the Commission's recommendations hastened the introduction of Canada's pioneering multicultural policy, which was announced in 1971 by Prime Minister Pierre Elliot Trudeau (for an overview of the history of multiculturalism in Canada, see Dewing and Leman 2006).

2 For example, in Australia, the Department of Immigration and Multicultural Affairs (DIMA) was renamed as the Department of Immigration and Citizenship in January 2007 by Australian Prime Minister John Howard, who saw this as 'not designed to kick multiculturalism, [but rather as] designed to better reflect the pathway to becoming an Australian inherent in a vibrant immigration program.' ('Howard drops multiculturalism', news.com.au 23 January 2007, <http://www.news.com.au/story/0,23599,21105650–1702,00. html> [last accessed 23.01.07]. In the case of Canada, the country hailed as the first to make multiculturalism a national official policy in 1971, a full-fledged Department of Multiculturalism and Citizenship was created in 1991, only to be dismantled and integrated two years later into the Department of Heritage portfolio (Dewing and Leman 2006). In the US, state programmes and practices aimed at the integration of minorities and the respect of cultural difference have retreated back in favour of more assimilationist practices and policies (Alba and Nee 2003; Brubaker 2003; Joppke and Morawska 2003; Mitchell 2004). In his State of the Union address of January 2007, President George W. Bush reiterated the 'need to uphold the great tradition of the melting pot that welcomes and assimilates new arrivals.' (see <http://www.whitehouse. gov/news/releases/2007/01/20070123–2.html> [last accessed 30.01.07]).

3 I am taking my cue, here, from Franklin, Lury and Stacey's (2000) analysis of globalization which they conceive as a project rather than an accomplished fact.

4 On 7 July 2005, four British Muslim men committed suicide in a concerted attack on the London transport system, killing 52 people and injuring 700.

5 Sarah Ahmed writes that in Australia, it is about the 'proximity of strangers' (2000: 95 *inter alia*). But as will hopefully become clear later in this chapter, the British version of multiculturalism differs from the Australian one if only as a result of their different colonial histories.

6 See Hage (2003) who develops 'care' as an analytical category to think about immigrant settlement and to expand on notions of citizenship to include the affective dimension of belonging.

7 For example, 'ethnic' community cohesion is deemed dysfunctional because it is too self-centred; see Chapter 4.

8 Melancholia is not a feature of contemporary Britain alone. See Weber 1999 on melancholia in US neo-imperial international politics, and Butler 2004 on US post 9/11 national melancholia. Other authors have sought in melancholia a way to explore the psychological dimensions of how we are socialized into 'race' (Cheng 2001; Eng and Han 2003) in ways that are directly related to past and present colonial histories and politics. Ranjanna Khanna (2006), for her part, discusses how the field of post-colonial studies is itself melancholic.

9 A key characteristic of melancholia, according to Freud, is 'an extraordinary diminution of [the melancholic's] self-regard, an impoverishment of his ego on a grand scale. In mourning it is the world which has become poor and empty; in melancholia it is the ego itself' (1957: 246). Thus, Freud suggests a narcissistic identification with the lost love-object; one where ego sees him or herself reflected in the love-object. What is being mourned then is not so much the loss of the love-object itself, but of ego (Freud 1957: 247). However, Freud adds that ambivalence is where melancholia takes hold; that is that the unresolved tension within the ambivalent love-hate relationship between ego and the love-object will cast mourning into a melancholic state where ego blames him or herself for the loss of the love-object. Hence the love-hate oscillation remains directed not at the love-object but at ego. I loved myself through her, but I hate her/myself for having lost her; and I hate that which in myself has led to that loss.

10 Some interventions have stressed the interconnections of race, ethnicity and class (Back 1996; Haylett 2001; Hewitt 2005), and feminist interventions have stressed the interconnections of race, ethnicity, and gender in multiculturalist politics (Ang 2001; Anthias and Yuval-Davis 1992; Bannerji 2000; Cohen *et al.* 1999). Overall, however, questions of kinship remain surprisingly absent.

11 Williams chose the term 'feeling' 'to emphasize a distinction from more formal concepts of "world-view" or "ideology"' (Williams in Hendler 2001: 10), thus underscoring 'the indeterminacy of emotions' (Berezin 2002: 39) as well as the 'affective processes that make up everyday life' (Hendler 2001: 11). Williams was concerned with 'meanings and values as they are actively lived and felt' (1977: 132) but 'without losing sight of how even these unevenly developed processes are mediated and structured' (Hendler 2001: 11). Williams establishes a clear distinction between what he calls the 'formal and systematic beliefs' (1977: 132) as they are codified in various sites, and the lived experience of these beliefs. What interests me in particular is how the 'lived experiences' are perceived and imagined as sources of concern or not, and in need of corrective measures that lead to the systematization and codification of feelings that become constitutive of 'formal and systematic beliefs'.

12 See Roger Hewitt's (2005) thoughtful account of how national narratives of multiculturalism influence local 'backlash' narratives among white Londoners.

13 This is not to say that fantasy is to utopia what the 'real' is to dystopia. Fantasies can carry positive or negative ideas and images – for example, the war on terror that distinguishes between evil terrorists and godly defenders of democracy necessarily relies on imaginings of destruction and evil which, although they are projected onto 'others' out there, are necessary to sustain the consistency and wholeness of the self (such as the 'American' national self, *or* Al Qaeda's religious self; indeed, similar fantasy frames operate on all sides of the war on terror and are not the prerogative of Western leaders. Bin Laden's colonizing mission is similarly divided between the evil forces of the West and the

blessed martyrs of jihad.) The war on terror relies on this sense of reality that clearly separates the other from the 'us', whereby the other's evil shores up 'our' godliness in order to sustain and make intelligible the inconsistency of engaging in acts of terror, be they against the US, Britain, or against Afghanistan, Iraq, and Iran. In this sense, fantasy ensures the wholeness of the subject and conceals its own ambivalence, inconsistencies, and splits, by projecting them onto others outside of itself. One of the issues considered in Chapter 3 is what happens to the national fantasy when the enemy is found within the national self, and the various mechanisms of expulsion and separation that are deployed to preserve the national whole.

14 One might be reminded of Homi Bhabha's theoretical moves in his classic essay 'DissemiNation' (1990), where he distinguishes between the pedagogical and performative elements in the construction of the nation. His conception of the nation/al as split between the performative and the pedagogical, suggests 'a shift in perspective that emerges from the nation's interrupted address, articulated in the tension signifying the people as *a priori* historical presence, a pedagogical object; and the people constructed in the performance of narrative, its enunciatory "present" marked in the repetition and pulsation of the national sign' (1990: 298–9). For Bhabha, the split erupts in that tension between the narrative authority of a people as originary and self-generating, on the one hand, and, on the other hand, the performative effects of signification that mark the nation Self, not as self-generating, but rather as constituted in *relation* to, and often against a constitutive Other or Outside. This split lies at the heart of that 'ambivalent identification of love and hate that binds a community together' (1990: 300). Bhabha's intervention crucially drew attention to 'the narcissistic neuroses of the national discourse' (1990: 300) that results from the collapse of the firm boundaries between Self and Other. But Bhabha, as well as Hesse, takes as his starting point the definition of the modern nation as mono-cultural and mono-ethnical. As I argue here, and throughout this book, different issues arise once the nation is conceived as inherently multicultural, and when the project is to achieve integration with diversity.

15 See Appadurai (1996), Hesse (1999), Stoetzler and Yuval-Davis (2002).

16 I am indebted to Michael Herzfeld's (1997) concept of 'cultural intimacy' for its emphasis on the interplay of local and national in definitions of the national culture – an interplay that is founded on 'the familiarity with the bases of power that may at one moment assure the disenfranchised a degree of creative irreverence and at the next moment reinforce the effectiveness of intimidation' (1997: 3).

17 With its class, racial, and gendered foundations inherited from English metropolitan and colonial histories, civility is related to ideas of civilization and progress, to moral ethical ideals of orderliness and good conduct, and to political conceptions of citizenship and participation in public institutions. Civility is to be understood in terms of surveillance, subjection, prescription, and inscription (Bhabha in Roy 2005: 9), which are at the foundation of its historical emergence as a site of making and unmaking the identity and alterity of the imperial/national culture as well as of the colonized/minoritized people (Bhabha 1985; Roy 2005).

18 The Commission is a fixed term advisory body set up in 2006, almost a year after the attacks in London in July 2005, with the mandate to consider 'how local areas can make the most of the benefits delivered by increasing diversity – [as well as to] consider how they can respond to the tensions it can sometimes cause. It will develop practical approaches that build communities' own capacity to prevent problems, including those caused by segregation and the dissemination of extremist ideologies'. From the Communities and Local

Government website <http://www.communities.gov.uk/index.asp?id = 1501520> [last accessed 06.02.07].

19 Seshadri-Crooks's distinction between 'White' with a capital 'W', and 'white' with a lowercase 'w' draws a useful line between 'Whiteness' as 'a discourse of difference which institutes a regime of looking' (2000: 97), and 'white' as 'a property of particular human beings' (2000: 97). However, in my attempts to sustain this distinction in the rest of this volume, I found it increasingly difficult to maintain a clear usage of 'Whiteness' with a capital 'W' without it appearing as a reification of the category as a fixed, non-relational and a-historical 'Thing' (this points to a broader discussion about the contributions and limits of a psychoanalytic framework, which is beyond the remit of this volume). In addition, the distinction between 'property', on the one hand, and a way of seeing the world, on the other, is not always easy to draw. Hence for these reasons, and to avoid confusion, the terms 'white' and 'whiteness' will be in lowercase from hereon except where referring specifically to Whiteness as a scopic regime, following Seshadri-Crooks (2000).

20 It is worth noting that among the chorus of new multiculturalists, Tory and Labour politicians were singing from the same hymn sheet in 2000. The former Tory leader William Hague stated that 'Britain is a nation of immigrants' (Hague 2000), while the once hard-line Conservative Michael Portillo appealed for tolerance at the Tory Party conference in October 2000: 'We are for all Britons', he declared, 'Black Britons, British Asians, white Britons. Britain is a country of rich diversity' (in White 2000).

21 I am reminded here of Ghassan Hage's (1998, Chapter 4) apt metaphor of the multicultural stew, but to which all ingredients are not added in the same proportion, in contrast to the melting-pot metaphor (see Sollors 1986, Chapter 3). Rather, the secret to the successful multicultural stew is the good balance of ingredients – a pinch of this, a little more of that – with no particular ingredient standing out.

22 Richard Weight (2002), among others, shows how the definition of Englishness has preoccupied numerous academics, journalists, and politicians since the beginning of the twentieth century. But the distinctive feature of the second half of that century is how definitions of Englishness, and more recently Britishness, are rethought and contested in direct relation to the impact of immigration.

2 Pride, shame, and the skin of citizenship

1 I refer to the English press by way of distinguishing it from Scottish, Welsh, Irish newspapers. The papers analyzed here all emanate from London, though they have the status of 'national newspapers' (*Guardian, Times, Telegraph, Daily Mail, Daily Mirror, Express, Sun*). Specifying their Englishness is meant to disentangle the conflation between Englishness and Britishness, where the former stands in for the latter. The material used here was compiled by Jennie Germann Molz in an electronic newspaper archive on multicultural Britain (October 2000 to May 2001), thanks to the financial support of the Faculty of Arts and Social Sciences (then the Faculty of Social Sciences) at Lancaster University. Jennie did a fantastic job at creating an exhaustive and user-friendly archive.

2 After the chair of the Commission, Professor Bhiku Parekh.

3 Moreover, in contrast to earlier versions of hybrid Englishness, the geography of 'new Britain', conceived as part of a globalized world, includes multilocal or translocal terrains of belonging that would be worth exploring in more detail elsewhere. This differs to colonial times, when Englishness was defined in its relation to colonies, but in a relationship of contrast and opposition, and one where here and there were clearly demarcated.

4 The relationship between Englishness and Britishness remains slippery throughout these debates, and would deserve a more detailed consideration than I can
do here. If at times Englishness stands in for Britishness, at other times the
emphasis on Britishness is precisely intended to open up the notion of Britishness and to disentangle it from Englishness. This is the Parekh Report's project,
which I return to later in this chapter.

5 This was the title of a report aired on the Discovery Channel in July 2003, and
fronted by Eddie Izzard, a popular British comedian, that celebrated 'Mongrel
Britain'. See also Dodd (1995) for an earlier positive use of the term.

6 To be sure, there are variations across the political spectrum, and not all accept
that Britishness is inherently multicultural (c.f. C. Johnson 2002). However, the
point here is that 'multiculturalism' and diversity were almost unanimously mobilized
as signs of British tolerance, against perceived accusations of national racism.

7 A distinctive feature of the report was its 'academic' groundings. Parekh himself
is an internationally-established political theorist, and other academics, such as
Stuart Hall, were on the commission. Its preliminary chapters were informed by
theoretical references to nation-building, including Anderson's (1991) 'imagined
communities', or to the politics of recognition (Taylor 1994). Predictably, this
was the subject of some of the hostility against the report. One *Sun* reader asked
why 'ordinary people' weren't 'invited to sit on commissions' (McSweeney 2000).

8 The coverage of the Report was not homogeneous. The *Express*, for example,
welcomed the Parekh Report and insisted that 'damning a report which highlights the problems' of racial prejudice was not the way forward (in Neal 2003:
73n3). There were some contrasting views between newspapers, but also some
ambivalence within newspapers themselves, such as in the *Guardian*. The
response discussed here, then, is not meant to be fully representative of the
printed media's coverage of the Parekh Report, but rather to explore in detail
the underlying issues in rejecting the Parekh Report.

9 Islington, in North London, has been associated with middle-class Labour sup-
porters and party members for several years. When Thatcher was Prime Minister, the Islington Borough Council was one of those she described as run by the
'loony left'. Today, it is still often dismissively associated with the 'chattering'
middle-class intellectuals. Tony and Cherie Blair and their family were residents
of Islington prior to their move to 10 Downing Street in 1997.

10 The Labour party even appointed their own 'patriotism envoy' in Michael
Wills, whose task was to encourage other members of the government to pay
special respect to British national identity in their speeches and, whenever possible, in their policy decisions. He was quoted in the *Telegraph* as saying that
the Parekh Report was 'profoundly wrong', that Britishness is an inclusive
category and there is no need to rework British history, since 'we have a history
and I do not think it is alienating' (in C. Johnson 2002: 168).

11 We could distinguish between guilt and shame: the former being a sentiment
that 'references an act or deed rather than a state of personhood' (Gunaratnam
and Lewis 2001: 143) and therefore 'is easier to get rid of' (Probyn 2005: 2). Shame,
for its part, is a deeply internalized emotion, 'an experience of the self by the
self' (Tomkins 1995: 137), which could result from, but is not reducible to, the
guilt for the immorality of a particular act. But what interests me here are the
issues at stake in the treatment of guilt and shame as equally repulsive affects.

12 As Mark Leonard remarked, Tony Blair is determined 'to seize the flag from the
Conservative Party' (2002: xi).

13 Kelly Holmes subsequently won two gold medals in the Athens Olympics of 2004.

14 At the time of the Athens Olympics of 2004, seventeen-year-old British Pakistani Muslim Amir Khan from Bolton became Britain's 'multi-cultural hero' after
winning a silver medal in boxing. Thus a detailed reading would be called for

here to explore the ways in which Holmes (called Britain's 'golden girl' after her achievement of two gold medals in Athens) and Khan were differently positioned as representatives of Britain in 2004 and, more broadly, how this relates to the re-positioning of West Indians, Asians and Muslims in the changing multicultural and multiracial landscape of contemporary Britain. I elaborate on such changes in the following two chapters, but not in relation to the sports scene.

15 In August 2005, the general outcry against Home Office minister Hazel Blear's consideration for 're-branding' ethnic minorities as hyphenated identities (British-Muslim, British-Pakistani, British-Jamaican) was a further indication of the post-ethnic aspirations for Britishness. Blear's idea was short lived and soon disappeared from public debates, in favour of finding ways to foster more pride in Britishness among Britain's minoritized populations, especially Muslim youth.

3 'Children of multicultural Britain': The good, the bad, the uncanny

1 This was the conclusion most journalists drew (with the exception of Hartley 2001) from Dorley-Brown's estimation, stated at the press conference, that his sample might have included 50 individuals from ethnic minorities (personal conversation with Chris Dorley-Brown, February 2002).

2 In 1993, *Time* magazine produced a similar national figure, the 'New Face of America', which was also the result of morphing technology, and was released in a similar context of assessing a new future in relation to a multicultural present. A number of scholars have written incisive observations about 'SimEve', as Donna Haraway (1997: 232 *inter alia*) christened her. These include Berlant 1997; Castañeda 2002; Hammonds 1997; Haraway 1997. These analyses have inspired my reading of 'the face of Britain', and have helped me identify the specificities that distinguish it from SimEve.

3 Lauren Berlant's analysis of infantile citizenship in the US has been somewhat influential in the development of my thinking here. Though her analysis centres on how US citizenship is infantilized, she also highlights the use of the child figure as iconic of 'the ideal type of patriotic personhood in America ... on whose behalf national struggles are being waged' (1997: 21). But my discussion is not so much about the infantilization of citizenship, nor is it about the ways in which state protectionism is founded on the iconic infantile citizen. Rather, I focus on the multicultural youth as she/he stands in for the successes, failures, and limits of multiculturalism.

4 Alexandra Dobrowolsky (2002: 44) points out that the figure of the child in New Labour rhetoric and policies is to be situated within a broader shift away from the welfare state to the 'social investment state', where the state spends on its citizens, but the spending is 'costed, calculated ... highly strategic' and is conditional to citizens fulfilling their responsibilities. In this rationale, 'spending on children now can help to improve a nation's long-term productive potential' (Dobrowolsky 2002: 44).

5 My understanding of 'figures' and 'figurations' comes from Donna Haraway's (1997) and Claudia Castañeda's definitions of figurations as compressions of material-semiotic practices that entail 'a specific configuration of knowledge, practice and power' that 'also [bring] a particular [yet contestable] world into being' (Castañeda 2002: 3). Although the figures discussed here are actual images of 'faces', it should not be concluded that figurations are reducible to such a literal translation. Nor are these images to be seen as mere 'figures', i.e. 'visual representations'. Rather, 'figurations' and 'figures' are materialized in different ways, and are assemblages of numerous practices of knowledge. For example, conceptions of 'youth' result from the assemblages of various practices and knowledges (psychological, medical, political, cultural, moral),

while 'youth' also works as a category that brings forth particular versions of the world (e.g. 'ethnic minority youth' as caught between two cultures, or as doubly disaffected, or as bridging agents between generations) that may be at the basis of strategies that are oriented towards 'youth' as members of wider communities (such as 'linking projects' that bus children between different faith schools). So, in some way, we could consider each figure here as a practice of representation, while it also does some work that also leads to other practices; in this sense, '[f]iguration is thus understood here to incorporate a double force: constitutive effect and generative circulation' (Castañeda 2002: 3).

6 The phrase comes from the title of an article by Tamsin Blanchard (2001) in the *Observer*, and discussed in the first section of this chapter.

7 I am aware that in the US, the acronym 'FOB' connotes 'fresh off the boat'. It is not my intention to attach this connotation to the nickname I attribute to the Face of Britain. Thanks to Eithne Luibheid for informing me of this.

8 He declared that 'Chicken Tikka Massala is now a true British national dish, not only because it is the most popular, but because it is a perfect illustration of the way Britain absorbs and adapts external influences. Chicken Tikka is an Indian dish. The Massala sauce was added to satisfy the desire of British people to have their meat served in gravy.' (21 April 2001; cited in <http://search.csmonitor.com/durable/2001/04/26/fp8s1-csm.shtml> [last accessed 2 March 2004]).

9 Morphing was devised in the mid-1800s by Francis Galton (1822–1911), Charles Darwin's cousin, as a technique for producing composite photographs from standardized portraits, with which he would record 'ideal-typical features' from large groups of people (convicts, the 'insane', public-school boys, Jews, and so on). A key precursor in the development of 'social Darwinism', Galton's techniques served to develop a theory about human degeneration, and were used to support his eugenics project of separating out the 'degenerate' elements from the rest of society to prevent them from procreating and from 'contaminating' the 'race' (Hamilton and Hargreaves 2001: 95–98). The work of Francis Galton and of some of his contemporaries was the subject of an exhibition, at the National Portrait Gallery in London in 2001, on the use of photography as a form of policing and constructing identities. Hanging on the wall next to the entrance to the exhibition room was Dorley-Brown's photograph, presented as a testimony to the contemporary legacy of the nineteenth-century invention. But the connections made between Dorley-Brown and Galton were strictly techno-logical: as I show in this chapter, Dorley-Brown's project is perceived as inclu-sive rather than differentialist due to its purported culturally diverse make-up.

10 Digital morphing was used in films such as *Terminator 2: Judgement Day* (1991), *Star Trek VI: The undiscovered country* (1991), and famously in Michael Jackson's video *Black or White* (1991); see Wolf (2000) for a summary of the history of morphing technology.

11 Visitors to the Haverhill 2000 website (<http://www.haverhill2000.com>) can witness the morphing of two images and progress through the 'generations' of morphs leading to the final morph that is FoB.

12 Part of the 'National Heritage' project, which 'celebrate[d] the methods of an "ignorant" and "filthy" London street culture.' See their website at <http://www.mongrel.org.uk/> [last accessed 12.02.07]. I am grateful to Nina Wakeford for drawing my attention to this project and for providing me with the Colour Separation poster.

13 These are the words of Graeme Harwood, one of the founding members of Mongrel, cited on the Colour Separation web page <http://www.mongrel.org.uk/?q = colourseparation> [last accessed 12.02.07].

14 Likewise, the Dorley-Brown portrait was starkly different to its predecessor Galton's work shown at the National Portrait Gallery in 2001 (see note 9

above). The nineteenth-century composites looked liked the superimposition of two or more ghostly figures where the silhouettes of different figures could be delineated and distinguished from each other. The eerie photographs could also be read as revealing the extent to which reality is inhabited by ghosts that could not be simply confined to the realm of superstition (cf. Gordon 1997).

15 My thanks to Cynthia Weber for this succinct and evocative way of describing morphing technologies.

16 Conversation with Nick Keeble, from Haverhill Town Council, November 2001.

17 Personal communication from the founder of the EMMA awards, Bobby Syed (14.11.06). Unfortunately, I was unable to reproduce the image discussed here because of prohibitive costs. The image can be found on the EMMA website <http://www.emma.tv/> [last accessed 12.02.07]. It will remain there, Syed assured me, throughout the period of EMMA's desired objective of 'promoting multiculturalism'. However, he did not specify how long that period would be.

18 In the UK, (mostly young) people wearing hooded sweatshirt are known as hoodies and have recently been associated with working class 'chav' culture. In May 2005, the largest shopping centre in the UK, Bluewater in Kent, caused outrage by releasing a code of conduct which bans its shoppers from sporting hoodies or baseball caps. Tony Blair supported the shopping centre's decision and promised to 'help restore "respect" for other people' (White 2005). Blair announced his 'respect' agenda in January 2006.

19 The burkha comes in many variations, but in its most conservative form it completely covers the face of the person wearing it, leaving only a mesh-like screen to see through.

20 The niqab (or nikab) covers everything below the bridge of the nose and the upper cheeks, and sometimes also covers the forehead.

21 A full-length loosely-fitted dress that conceals a woman's arms and legs, and worn with a tightly fitting headscarf, or hijab, around the head and shoulders.

22 See also Ahmed (2004: 136) for a short discussion of Blanchard's article.

23 However this has not always been the case. Social histories of migration and nation formation reveal how the meanings of difference and the boundaries of 'race' change in space and time; we can only remember how Irish or Italian migrants 'became white' in the US (Ignatiev 1996; Roediger 1991, 1994). As I point out elsewhere (2000: Chapter 2), labels of 'white ethnics' (in the US) and 'white negroes' (in the UK) attributed to some immigrant populations (such as Italians or Irish) testify to different forms of articulations of race, culture, class, and nation and, crucially, to the variability of whiteness and of the ways in which whiteness is seen.

24 Andrew Marr, former BBC political editor, member of the Commission on the Future of Multi-Ethnic Britain (CFMEB 2000), and influential political commentator, wrote in his book *The Day Britain Died* (2000) that England will thrive only if it embraces the cultural mélange that could result from its present diversity, and that descendants of 'non-white communities' will play a significant role in this development: 'Quite a few people who are going to shape our lives over the next 50 years are children today who do not speak English as their first tongue and are struggling in inner-city schools. There will be, somewhere out there, a Black Thatcher, and Albanian Mick Jagger and a Chinese David Hockney – and maybe, if we are lucky, a Bangladeshi Bill Gates' (2000a: 162). For Marr, the expected success of dark-skinned allophones is paving the way to the nation's future, promising a new future for Britain and Britons. There is something special about today's minorities in Marr's view: something that gives special force and velocity to the immigrants' cultural practices, which are changing people's everyday lives in a radical way. And that something is

marked in terms of skin colour and language, on the one hand, and lifestyle, on the other. And that something, that *future*, is hybrid.

25 The 'mixed' category in the 2001 census included: 'White and Black Caribbean', 'White and Black African', 'White and Asian', 'Any other mixed background' (Owen 2001: 146).

26 Barnbrook was attending the English National Ballet's production of 'Giselle' on Friday 12 January 2007, in support of the lead dancer Simone Clarke, for whom it was the first public performance since the *Guardian* named her as a member of the BNP during an investigation into the far-right organisation. The *Guardian* reported that 'Mr Barnbrook ... said she had his full backing and that he did not object to her relationship with Cuban-Chinese dancer Yat-Sen Chang. "She's not racist – she's going out with someone who is not of her own race," he said. But he said, he hoped the couple would not have children' (in Taylor 2007).

27 Similarly, Andrew Marr states, hopefully, that though 'over time today's new British will slowly mingle with the old British, but the rate of intermarriage is still tiny' (2000a: 155).

28 See Spickard (2001) on the rise of mixed-race celebrities and of the popularity of mixed-race literature.

29 He is currently serving a life sentence at the ADX Florence, a Supermax prison in Florence, Colorado.

30 It is noteworthy that Hussain's photograph is absent in the *Guardian* article discussed here. The photo that was released in the national press in the summer of 2005 looked like a passport photo. Full frontal, unsmiling, undecipherable, it could also be a mug shot. This photograph is not of the family-album type. Hussain's unsmiling face has nothing of the sweet, schoolboy picture of Shehzad Tanweer, or of the happy family picture of Germaine Lindsay with his wife and young child. Not surprising, then, that Hussain's 'portrait' was put into words only in the *Guardian* article: it said what the photograph could not. Hussain's photograph appears on several websites – a simple Google search will lead you to one of them.

31 See <http://news.bbc.co.uk/2/hi/uk_news/4678837.stm> [last accessed 05.04.07].

32 I could not locate this photograph on any website, but it was printed along with the photographs of the other three men, in the *Observer* on 17 July 2005: 15.

33 Kuhn is writing, here, about the 'naked and immaculate body of the newborn' baby (2002: 51). I believe there are parallels, however, in the school photograph, with its formulaic format as well as with the generic school-uniform, that make children's bodies into some kind of 'naked' blank slate.

34 Repetition is for Freud a feature of the uncanny. He writes that in the uncanny, 'there is a constant recurrence of the same thing – the repetition of the same features or character-traits or vicissitudes, of the same crimes, or even the same names through several consecutive generations' (Freud 1955: 234).

35 On Thursday 10 August 2006, fourteen men and one woman (later released) were arrested under suspicion of this alleged plot. As a result, both the UK and the US immediately stepped up security in airports, following the revelation of the plot which was believed to involve a 'liquid chemical' device. As in July 2005, narratives about the ordinariness of the lives of the suspects widely circulated in the national press.

36 Since 7/7, Tony Blair has consistently refused to make any connections between the UK's international policies in the Middle East and the anger of young British Muslims. Similarly, some researchers have blamed British multiculturalism – not British international policies – as the root-cause of Islamic terrorism. For example, in January 2007, the independent think-tank Policy Exchange published the results of a survey about attitudes of Muslims in Britain. One of its

conclusions is that one of the reasons behind the rapid rise of Islamic fundamentalism among younger generations is 'in part, a result of multicultural policies implemented since the 1980s which have emphasised difference at the expense of shared national identity and divided people along ethnic, religious and cultural lines' (Mirza *et al.* 2007: 6).

37 Will Hutton is a well-known economist and author who was formerly editor-in-chief of the *Observer* and economics editor of the *Guardian*, and continues to write regular columns in the *Observer*. He has also worked as economics correspondent for radio and television, where he is now an occasional commentator.

38 It is beyond the scope of this chapter to discuss the fragmentation of 'minorities' along the lines of 'old' and 'new' migrations, 'settled communities', and 'faith communities', and the shifting subject positions and subjectivities that are constituted through these distinctions. See Lewis (2006b).

39 Broken-backed (or brokenbacked) also has homophobic connotations and has been used to deride men as effeminate, and at times conveys general contempt. Whether Hutton is aware of such uses is unknown, but these connotations are noteworthy when we consider the heterosexual foundations of the national fantasy. Thanks to Cindy Weber for drawing this to my attention; see Zwicky (2006) on colloquial uses of the term and its various gendered and sexual meanings.

4 Loving thy neighbour and the politics of inter-ethnic propinquity

1 Thompson was director and producer. The film was a Mentorn production. For information, see the Mentorn website: <http://www.mentorn.co.uk/Programmes/? pid = 4&id = 24&vid = 65> [last accessed 12.01.07]

2 A Tory MP at the time, Enoch Powell gave his 'Rivers of Blood Speech' in Birmingham in 1968. In the speech he suggested that black crime was at the centre of a range of 'problems' caused by immigration. Powell used the example of a terrified elderly widow, the last white resident in her street, being taunted by young black Caribbean boys, to illustrate the threats posed by immigration (see Smithies and Fiddick, 1969: 41–42). Though Powell's 1960s Birmingham is not today's Bradford, the legacies of Powellism ring through the trope of the last white household surrounded by 'foreigners'. It is worth adding that the households that figured in both Powell's speech and Thompson's film are without a patriarchal 'head' (Sharon Gallagher is a single mother), and that this was indeed integral to the moral panic with which some reviewers met the film (discussed later in this chapter).

3 When we are introduced to the cousins, Devlin is the only one whose age is undisclosed; instead, we are informed that his 'dad is Jamaican'. Devlin is immediately positioned as 'mixed race', a point I return to later in this chapter.

4 In 1984, a local headmaster, Ray Honeyford, was forced out of his job for having suggested that white children were 'slowed down' in schools with a large Asian intake, prompting a white flight from frightened parents; in 1989, angry Muslim residents in Bradford staged book burnings of Salman Rushdie's *The Satanic Verses*; in 1995, young Pakistani men took to the streets and engaged in three days of public disorder that came to be known as 'The Bradford Riots'; the Bradford Riots followed other disturbances that took place earlier in 1995 during the local election campaign when two Muslim candidates from rival clans opposed each other, and further disturbances during an anti-prostitution campaign. See Mary Macey (1999) for a look at the changes from orderly to disorderly and violent public protest among Pakistani men in Bradford.

5 The term 'Muslim Asian' captures the conflation that occurs in the public domain between Islam and the South Asian population as a whole, while at the

same time the phrase seeks to act as a reminder that Islamophobia is at the heart of the issue. However, the term 'Muslim Asian' might be another generalization insofar as Pakistanis are often specifically targeted in racist attacks and verbal abuse. In turn, 'Paki' has come to be used as a generic derogative term for all South Asians. I use 'Muslim Asian' or 'Asian' when the discourses I analyze effect that conflation, but also to note how entire populations – be they Muslim or Asian – are homogenized. I apologize in advance to readers who might feel vexed by my use of this phrase and can only hope that we can open a discussion about what constitutes appropriate terminology that captures the points of convergence between groups without losing sight of the specificity of their historicity and locatedness.

6 Can the experiences of Asians and Caribbeans be aligned to those of Jews or Irish? How is whiteness at play? Indeed, how and when did the Catholic and perhaps Irish background of the Gallagher family become elided into Englishness (in the film, Sharon Gallagher, the mother, refers to her Catholic background and identifies as English)? In present day Britain, 'ethnics' are differently positioned in a multicultural landscape that is cast within the wider frame of national security and European expansion. I address this later in the chapter in relation to the distinction between 'settled' communities of the 'old' migration, and 'new' migrants (see Lewis 2006b for an insightful look at the current conjuncture).

7 In October 2006, the government backed down from introducing an amendment to the Education and Inspections Bill that would have enabled local councils to require new faith schools to select up to 25 per cent of their intake from pupils of other faith backgrounds or those with no religious beliefs. Following talks with representatives of major religious groups in the UK, the then Education Secretary Alan Johnson announced that a voluntary agreement had been reached. The result is that schools will not be assessed for their actual intake of pupils of a different or no faith, but rather for their commitment to community cohesion. As Muslim leaders reportedly pointed out, although their schools allow for 20 per cent to 25 per cent of places to be taken up by non-Muslim pupils, few people take up the opportunity. See 'Faith schools quota plan scrapped', <http://news.bbc.co.uk/1/hi/education/6089440.stm> [last accessed 06.03.07].

8 My thanks to Gail Lewis for this suggestion.

9 Though her book is about queer belongings and not diasporic ones, Probyn's (1996) phrase is apposite here.

10 Only one reviewer, from *The Independent on Sunday*, refers to Sharon Gallagher in a markedly positive way, saying she is 'admirable' – though he does not specify why (I. Millar 2003).

11 This and the previous quote come from <http://www.respect.gov.uk/article.aspx?id = 9066> [last accessed 05.03.07].

12 The large body of research on mixed-race children has long since explored similar questions and discussed the ways in which 'mixed race' is a form of critique, a way of discrediting racial categories and the social meanings of 'race'. See for example Ali (2003); Ifekwunigwe (1999); Parker and Song (2001a).

13 Sara Ahmed reports how 'the British National Party's response to September 11 was to posit Islamicisation within the UK rather than the Taliban in Afghanistan as the threat to the moral future of the nation itself: "They can turn Britain into an Islamic Republic by 2025"' (2004: 77).

14 In Bradford, for example, national authorities obtained the guarantee that ethnic leaders would contain and cover up ethnic minority resistance in exchange for their withdrawal from 'internal affairs', namely the highly contentious

issue of forced marriages (Amin 2002; Kundnani 2001; Macey 1999; Sahgal 2002). This kind of 'integration' sustains systems of inequalities within, as well as between, communities, in the name of cultural preservation.

5 How does it feel? Feeling states and the limits of the civil nation

1 In May 2006, celebrity chef Worral Thompson was reported in the *Daily Telegraph* as complaining about Eastern European waiters and waitresses working in English restaurants because they 'did not speak enough English to do the job properly and [he] suggested scrapping the minimum wage in order to encourage staff to raise their game in the hope of receiving tips' (Cramb 2006).

2 I am informed here by recent developments in feminist and cultural theory, as well as earlier works in socio-psychology, that question the privatization of feeling as simply a feature on individual psyches (Ahmed 2004; Berlant 2004; Brennan 2004; Cvetkovich 1992, 2003; Katz 1999; Probyn 2005; Sedgwick 2003).

3 In May 2002, singer, actor, and presenter Toyah Willcox wrote an article in the *Sunday Times*, in which she complained about a government plan to build an asylum centre in a small village of Worcestershire where her parents live. In the article, Willcox moved swiftly from embracing the lively presence of foreign fruit-pickers who come every year, which is signalled by the different languages heard at the village newsagent, to language becoming a barrier for those asylum-seekers who might be relocated there. This is an interesting example of how lively and *temporary* diversity becomes undesirable *permanent* difference. See Willcox (2002).

4 This was in August 2006. The quotes come form various media reports that circulated at the time. The two men were interviewed on the *Today* programme, BBC Radio 4, on 24 August 2006. They claimed they were not deliberately fooling around to arouse people's fear (as had been suggested) and that one was wearing a black fleece top, not the hefty black leather jacket that was reported. They were students in Manchester.

5 I am indebted to Jennie Germann Molz whose work on round-the-world travellers drew my attention to the ways in which feeling and not feeling borders can co-exist. Germann Molz writes about the tension, for travellers, between wanting to feel and not feel the national borders when they cross from one country to the other. Borders must be both permeable (so that travellers can pass through them easily), and, like the Equator or the International Date Line, marked or felt (so that the traveller has the physical evidence of the crossing). (See Germann Molz 2004.)

6 Brick Lane is a street in the East End of London and heart of an area known as Banglatown because of its large Sylheti Bangladeshi community. Brick Lane is also widely known as the location of different waves of migration through the years, beginning with the French Huguenot and Jewish migrations.

7 Andrew Marr was a member of the Commission on the Future of Multi-Ethnic Britain discussed in Chapter 2, but resigned when he was appointed political editor for the BBC. He is now a radio talk-show host for BBC radio 4's 'Start the Week'. At the beginning of 2000, before the Parekh Report was published, Marr presented a three-part television series for BBC2, based on his subsequently published book, *The Day Britain Died*, where he considers the future of Britain in the context of globalization, devolution, animal rights activism, anti-capitalist protests, and multiculture. Matthew Taylor, for his part, was visiting Brick Lane in the context of a television report about an ICN poll conducted with the Institute for Public Policy Research (IPPR) that explored what white Britons

think of multiculturalism. Taylor later became Chief Adviser on Strategy to Prime Minister Tony Blair.

8 Blair was commenting on Straw's remark, as well as on a case made by a teaching assistant, Aishah Azmi, against her local council that suspended her for refusing to remove the niqab in the classroom. Her claims of religious discrimination and harassment were rejected by the government's Employment Tribunal, though she was awarded £2,000 for victimization.

9 Fortuyn was a Dutch politician renowned for his Islamophobia and his hostility towards non-European immigration to the Netherlands. His arguments were founded on cultural difference as a source of conflict, and on the refusal to integrate on the part of numerous immigrants, especially Muslims. He was shot dead by an animal rights activist in May 2002.

10 This is the title of the citizenship test that some applicants for naturalization must take. It is also the title of the handbook produced by the Home Office to prepare applicants for the test. (See Home Office 2004b.)

Bibliography

Ackroyd, Peter (2002) *Albion: the Origins of the English Imagination*, London: Chatto.

Ahmad, Muneer (2002) 'Homeland insecurities: racial violence the day after September 11', *Social Text*, 20(3): 101–15.

Ahmed, Sara (1998) 'Tanning the body: skin, colour and gender', *New Formations*, 39: 27–42.

——(2000) *Strange Encounters. Embodied Others in Postcoloniality*, London: Routledge.

——(2004) *The Cultural Politics of Emotion*, Edinburgh: Edinburgh University Press.

Alba, Richard and Nee, Victor (2003) *Remaking the American Mainstream: Assimilation and Contemporary Immigration*, Cambridge, MA: Harvard University Press.

Alexander, Jacqui and Mohanty, Chandra Talpade (eds) (1997) *Feminist Genealogies Colonial Legacies. Democratic Futures*, New York: Routledge.

Alexander, Jeffrey C. (2001) 'Theorizing the "modes of incorporation": assimilation, hyphenation, and multiculturalism as varieties of civil participation', *Sociological Theory*, 19: 237–49.

Ali, Suki (2003) *Mixed-Race, Post-Race. Gender, New Ethnicities and Cultural Practices*, Oxford: Berg.

Amin, Ash (2002) 'Ethnicity and the multicultural city: living with diversity', *Environment and Planning A*, 34: 959–80.

Anderson, Benedict (1991) *Imagined Communities*, London and New York: Verso.

Ang, Ien (2001) *On Not Speaking Chinese. Living Between Asia and the West*, London: Routledge.

Anonymous (2001) 'The Face of Britain', *Daily Mail*, 30 March: 22.

Anthias, Floya and Yuval-Davis, Nira (1989) 'Introduction', in N. Yuval-Davis and F. Anthias (eds) *Woman-Nation-State*, London: Macmillan.

——(1992) *Racialized Boundaries: Race, Nation, Gender, Colour and Class and the Anti-Racist Struggle*, London: Routledge.

Appadurai, Arjun (1996) *Modernity at Large: Cultural Dimensions of Globalization*, Minneapolis: University of Minnesota Press.

Back, Les (2001) 'The Urgency of Becoming "Not White"', paper presented at the conference on *New European Identities: Race and Multiculturalism*, organized by the BSA sub-committee on 'race and ethnicity', School of Oriental and African Studies, London, 14 September 2001.

——(1996) *New Ethnicities and Urban Culture. Racisms and Multiculture in Young Lives*, London: UCL Press.

Back, Les, Crabbe, Tim and Solomos, John (2001) *The Changing Face of Football. Racism, Multiculturalism and Identity in the English Game*, Oxford: Berg.

Back, Les, Keith, Michael, Khan, Azra, Shukra, Kalbir and Solomos, John (2002) 'The Return of Assimilationism: race, multiculturalism and New Labour', *Sociological Research Online* 7(2). Available at: <http://www.socresonline.org.uk/7/2/back.html> [last accessed 4 June 2003].

Bale, Joanna (2001) 'Average faces add up to beauty', *Times*, 30 March 2001.

Bannerji, Himani (2000) *The Dark Side of the Nation. Essays on Multiculturalism, Nationalism and Gender*, Toronto: Canadian Scholars' Press.

Barbalet, Jack (2001) *Emotions, Social Theory, and Social Structure. A Macrosociological Approach*, Cambridge: Cambridge University Press.

Barthes, Roland (1980) *La chambre claire. Notes sur la photographie*, Paris: Gallimard Seuil.

——(1981) *Camera Lucida. Reflections on Photography*, trans. R. Howard, New York: Hill and Wang.

Baumann, Gerd (1999) *The Multicultural Riddle*, London: Routledge.

Beams, Nick (2004) 'What is at stake in Australia's "History Wars". Part 5: John Howard and "the Australian way of life"', *World Socialist Website*. Available at: <http://www.wsws.org/articles/2004/jul2004/hiw5-j16.shtml> [last accessed 23 January 2007].

Bedell, Geraldine (2003) 'Between two worlds', *Observer Review*, 6 April 2003.

Benedictus, Leo (2005) 'London: the world in one city', *Guardian*, 21 January 2005, Special pull-out.

Benjamin, Alison (2005) 'Harmony's Herald', *Guardian Unlimited*, 21 September 2005. Available at: <http://society.guardian.co.uk/interview/story/0,1574183,00.html> [last accessed 21 September 2005].

Bennett, David (1998) 'Introduction', in D. Bennett (ed.) *Multicultural States. Rethinking Difference and Identity*, London & New York: Routledge.

Berezin, Mabel (2002) 'Secure states: towards a political sociology of emotions', in J. Barbalet (ed.) *Emotions and Sociology*, Oxford: Blackwell.

Berlant, Lauren (1991) *The anatomy of National Fantasy: Hawthorne, Utopia and Everyday Life*, Chicago, IL: University of Chicago Press.

——(1997) *The Queen of America Goes to Washington City*, Durham, NC: Duke University Press.

——(2000) (ed.) *Intimacy*, Chicago, IL: University of Chicago Press, Chicago.

——(2001) 'Trauma and Ineloquence', *Cultural Values*, 5(1): 41–58.

——(ed.) (2004) *Compassion: the Culture and Politics of an Emotion*, London: Routledge.

Bhabha, Homi K. (1985) 'Sly Civility', *October*, 34: 71–80.

——(1990) 'DissemiNation: time, narrative, and the margins of the modern nation', in H. K. Bhabha (ed.) *Nation and Narration*, London: Routledge.

——(1994) *The Location of Culture*, London: Routledge.

Bhattacharyya, Gargi (1998) 'Riding Multiculturalism', in D. Bennett (ed.) *Multicultural States. Rethinking Difference and Identity*, London: Routledge.

Billig, Michael (1995) *Banal Nationalism*, London: Sage.

Blair, Tony (1996) *New Britain: My Vision for a Young Country*, London: Fourth Estate.

——(2000) Tony Blair's 'Britain Speech', *Guardian Unlimited*, 28 March 2000. Available at: <http://www.guardian.co.uk/britain/article/0,2763,184950,00.html> [last accessed 4 January 2005].

——(2006) 'Our Nation's Future – multiculturalism and integration', speech given at Downing Street on 8 December 2006. Available at: <http://www.number10.gov.uk/output/Page10563.asp> [last accessed 9 December 2006].

Blanchard, Tamsin (2001) 'Model of a modern Briton', *The Observer*, 25 November 2001, 'Race in Britain' Supplement: 10.

Blunkett, David (2001) 'Foreword', in Home Office *Secure Borders, Safe Haven. Integration with Diversity in Modern Britain*, London: Stationary Office CM 5387.

——(2002) 'Integration with diversity: globalisation and the renewal of democracy and civil society', in P. Griffith and M. Leonard (eds) *Reclaiming Britishness. Living Together After 11 September and the Rise of the Right*, London: Foreign Policy Centre.

Bourdieu, Pierre (1984) *Distinction: A Social Critique of the Judgement of Taste*, trans. R. Nice, London: Routledge & Kegan Paul.

Brennan, Teresa (2004) *The Transmission of Affect*, Ithaca, NY: Cornell University Press.

Brown, Gordon (2006) 'The Future of Britishness', keynote speech given at the Fabian Society *Future of Britishness* conference, 14 January 2006. Available at: < http://www.fabian-society.org.uk/press_office/display.asp?id = 520&type = news&cat = 43 > [last accessed 3 November 2006].

——(2007) 'We need a United Kingdom', *Daily Telegraph*, 13 January 2007. Available at: < http://www.telegraph.co.uk/news/main.jhtml?xml = /news/2007/01/13/ngordon113.xml > [last accessed 13 January 2007].

Brown, Wendy (2006) *Regulating Aversion. Tolerance in the Age of Empire and Identity*, Princeton: Princeton University Press.

Brubaker, Rogers (2003) '"The return of assimilation?" Changing perspectives on immigration and its sequels in France, Germany, and the United States', in C. Joppke and E. Morawska (eds) *Toward Assimilation and Citizenship: Immigrants in Liberal Nation-States*, Basingstoke: Palgrave Macmillan.

Burnley Task Force (2001) *Burnley Task Force*. Available at: <www.burnleytaskforce.org.uk> [last accessed 10 January 2002]

Butler, Judith (1997) *Excitable Speech. A Politics of the Performative*, London: Routledge.

——(2002) 'Is kinship always already heterosexual?', *Differences*, 13(1): 14–44.

——(2004) *Precarious Life. The Powers of Mourning and Violence*, London: Verso.

Callan, Paul (2004) 'Paul Callan – Column', *Sunday Express*, 29 February 2004.

Carrington, Ben (2000) 'Double consciousness and the Black British athlete', in K. Owusu (ed.) *Black British Culture and Society. A Text Reader*, London: Routledge.

Castañeda, Claudia (2002) *Figurations. Child, Bodies, Worlds*, Durham: Duke University Press.

CFMEB (Commission on the Future of Multi-Ethnic Britain) (2000) *The Future of Multiethnic Britain. The Parekh Report*, London: Profile Books.

Chakrabarty, Dipesh (2000) *Provincializing Europe: Postcolonial Thought and Historical Difference*, Princeton, NJ: Princeton University Press.

Chalmers, Sarah and Brooke, Chris (2003) 'The new ethnic minority', *Daily Mail*, 30 October 2003.

Chandran, Raj (2000) 'An insult to all our countrymen', *Daily Mail*, 11 October 2000.

Chatterjee, Partha (1986) *Nationalist Thought and the Colonial World*, London: Zed.

——(1993) *The Nation and its Fragments*, Princeton, NJ: Princeton University Press.

Cheng, Anne Anlin (2001) *The Melancholy of Race. Psychoanalysis, Assimilation, and Hidden Grief*, Oxford: Oxford University Press.

Chow, Rey (2002) *The Protestant Ethnic and the Spirit of Capitalism*, New York: Columbia University Press.

Clarkson, Frank (2000) letter published in the *Sun*, 'Big Issue' Section, 16 October 2000.

Cobain, Ian (2005) 'The bomber – Boy who didn't stand out', *Guardian*, 14 July 2005.

Cohen, Joshua, Howard, Matthew and Nussbaum, Martha C. (eds.) (1999) *Is Multiculturalism Bad for Women? Susan Moller Okin with Respondents*, Princeton: Princeton University Press.

Colley, Linda (2003) *Captives: Britain, Empire and the World 1600–1850*, London: Pimlico.

Cramb, Auslan (2006) 'Chef in the soup over jibe at Polish waiters', *Daily Telegraph*, 11 May 2006. Available at: <http://www.telegraph.co.uk/news/main. jhtml;jsessionid = P2JVL5CFILOQDQFIQMFSFGGAVCBQ0IV0?xml = /news/ 2006/05/11/nserv11.xml> [last accessed 11 May 2006].

CRCBB (Canadian Royal Commission on Bilingualism and Biculturalism) (1969) *Book Four: The Cultural Contribution of the Other Ethnic Groups*, Ottawa: Supply and Services Canada.

Crimp, Douglas (1989) 'Mourning and militancy', *October*, 51: 3–18.

Cvetkovich, Ann (1992) *Mixed Feeling: Feminism, Mass Culture and Victorian Sensationalism*, New Brunswick, NJ: Rutgers University Press.

——(2003) *An archive of Feelings: Trauma, Sexuality, and Lesbian Public Cultures*, Durham: Duke University Press.

de Lauretis, Teresa (1987) *Technologies of Gender: Essays on Theory, Film and Fiction*, London: Macmillan.

Derrida, Jacques (1997) *Politics of Friendship*, London: Verso.

Dewing, Michael and Leman, Mark (2006) *Canadian Multiculturalism*, Ottawa: Library of Parliament, Parliamentary Research Branch.

Dobrowolsky, Alexandra (2002) 'Rhetoric versus reality: The figure of the child and New Labour's strategic "social investment state"', *Studies in Political Economy*, 69: 43–73.

Dodd, Philip (1995) *The Battle Over Britain*, London: Demos.

Donald, James (1999) *Imagining the Modern City*, London: The Athlone Press.

Doughty, Steve (2000a) 'Racism slur on the word "British"', *Daily Mail*, 11 October 2000.

——(2000b) 'Blair's reversal on race', *Daily Mail*, 12 October 2000.

——(2000c) 'Why Charles should have chosen a black bride, by peer's wife', *Daily Mail*, 18 October 2000.

Dyer, Richard (1997) *White*, London: Routledge.

Edensor, Tim (2002) *National Identity, Popular Culture and Everyday Life*, Oxford: Berg.

Eller, Jack D. (1997) 'Anti-anti-multiculturalism', *American Anthropologist*, 99(2): 249–60.

Eng, David and Han, Shinhee (2003) 'A dialogue on racial melancholia', in D. Eng and D. Kazanjian (eds) *Loss. The Politics of Mourning*, Berkeley: University of California Press.

Ford, Richard (2000) '"Proud to be British" Straw raps race report', *Times*, 12 October 2000.

Fortier, Anne-Marie (2000) *Migrant Belongings: Memory, Space, Identity*, Oxford: Berg.

——(2006) 'The politics of scaling, timing and embodying: Rethinking the "New Europe"', *Mobilities*, 1(3): 313–31.

Foucault, Michel (1979) *The History of Sexuality*, Vol. 1, Harmondsworth: Penguin.

——(1997) *Il faut défendre la société*, Paris: Seuil/Gallimard.

Franklin, Sarah, Lury, Celia and Stacey, Jackey (2000) *Global Nature, Global Culture*, London: Routledge.

Freud, Sigmund (1955[1919]) 'The "uncanny"', in J. Strachey (ed.) *The Standard Edition of the Complete Psychological Works of Sigmund Freud*, Vol. 17, London: Hogarth.

——(1957[1917/1915]) 'Mourning and melancholia', in J. Strachey (ed.) *The Complete Psychological Works of Sigmund Freud*, Vol. 14, London: Hogarth Press and The Institute of Psycho-Analysis.

Frosh, Stephen, Phoenix, Ann and Pattman, Rob (2002) *Young Masculinities: Understanding Boys in Contemporary Society*, Basingstoke: Palgrave.

Furbank, Kevan (2000) 'We're all a little Brit of everything', *Daily Mirror*, 20 October 2000.

Gabriel, John (1998) *Whitewash. Racialized Politics and the Media*, London: Routledge.

Germann Molz, Jennie (2004) *Destination World: Technology, Mobility and Global Belonging in Round-the-World Travel Websites*, unpublished PhD thesis, Department of Sociology, Lancaster University.

Gibson, Owen, Dodd, Virkam and Ramesh, Randeep (2007) 'Racism, ratings and reality TV: Now Big Brother creates a diplomatic incident', *Guardian*, 18 January 2007. Available at: <http://www.guardian.co.uk/india/story/0,1992918,00.html> [last accessed 22 January 2007].

Gillan, Audrey (2005) 'The victim – Modern and still traditional', *Guardian*, 14 July 2005.

Gilroy, Paul (2001) 'Joined-up politics and post-colonial melancholia', *Theory, Culture & Society*, 18(2/3): 151–68.

——(2002) 'Diving into the tunnel: The politics of race between old and new worlds', *Open Democracy*, 31 January 2002. Available at: <www.openDemocracy.net> [last accessed 2 February 2002].

——(2003) '"Where ignorant armies clash by night". Homogenous community and the planetary aspect', *International Journal of Cultural Studies*, 6(3): 261–76.

——(2004a) *After Empire. Melancholia or Convivial Culture?*, Abingdon: Routledge.

——(2004b) 'Melancholia and multiculture', *Open Democracy*, 3 August 2004. Available at: <www.openDemocracy.net> [last accessed 8 August 2004].

Glazer, Nathan (1997) *We are All Multiculturalists Now*, Cambridge, MA: Harvard University Press.

Goldberg, David Theo (1994) 'Introduction: Multicultural Conditions', in D. T. Goldberg (ed.) *Multiculturalism. A Critical Reader*, Oxford: Blackwell.

Goodhart, David (2004) 'Discomfort of Strangers', *Guardian*, 24 February 2004.

Gordon, Avery F. (1997) *Ghostly Matters. Haunting and the Sociological Imagination*, Minneapolis: University of Minnesota Press.

Gorham, Clare (2003) 'Mixing it', *Guardian Weekend*, 22 February 2003.

Gregory, Derek (2004) *The Colonial Present. Afghanistan, Palestine, Iraq*, Oxford: Blackwell.

Grillo, Ralph and Pratt, Jeff (eds) (2002) *The Politics of Recognizing Difference. Multiculturalism Italian-Style*, Aldershot: Ashgate.

Gunaratnam, Yasmin (2006) '"And all they could hear was the screams ..." Acoustic space, excess and ethics in a multi-cultural hospice ward', Seminar presentation, Institute for Women's Studies, Lancaster University, Lancaster, 10 May 2006.

Gunaratnam, Yasmin and Gail Lewis (2001) 'Racialising emotional labour and emotionalising racialised labour: anger, fear and shame in social welfare', *Journal of Social Work Practice*, 15 (2): 131–48.

Gunew, Sneja (2004) *Haunted Nations. The Colonial Dimensions of Multiculturalisms*, London: Routledge.

Hage, Ghassan (1997) 'At home in the entrails of the West: Multiculturalism, ethnic food and migrant home-building', in H. Grace, G. Hage, L. Johnson, J. Langsworth and M. Symonds, *Home/World: Space, Community and Marginality in Sidney's West*, Sydney: Pluto Press.

——(1998) *White Nation. Fantasies of White Supremacy in a Multicultural Society*, Annandale, Australia, and West Whikham, UK: Pluto and Comerford & Miller.

——(2003) *Against Paranoid Nationalism. Searching for Hope in a Shrinking Society*, Annandale, Australia: Pluto.

Hague, William (2000) 'Why I am sick of the anti-British disease', *Daily Telegraph*, 13 October 2000.

Hall, Stuart (2000) 'Conclusion: The multi-cultural question', in B. Hesse (ed.) *Un/settled Multiculturalisms. Diasporas, Entanglements, Transruptions*, London: Zed Books.

Hamilton, Peter and Hargreaves, Roger (2001) *The Beautiful and the Damned. The Creation of Identity in Nineteenth-Century Photography*, Aldershot & London: Lund Humphries in association with The National Portrait Gallery.

Hammonds, Evelynn M. (1997) 'New technologies of race', in J. Terry & M. Calvert (eds) *Processed Lives. Gender and Technology in Everyday Life*, London: Routledge.

Haraway, Donna J. (1997) *Modest Witness @Second Millenium*, London: Routledge.

Harney, Nicholas de Maria (2006) 'The alternative economies of emigration and immigration, the Real and the constitution of Italian nation spaces', *Mobilities*, 1 (3): 373–90.

Hartley, Emma (2001) 'The face of Britain, digitally created', *Independent*, 30 March 2001.

Haylett, Chris (2001) 'Illegitimate subjects? Abject whites, neoliberal modernisation, and middle-class multiculturalism', *Environment and Planning D: Society and Space*, 19: 351–70.

Hendler, Glenn (2001) *Public Sentiments. Structures of Feeling in Nineteenth-Century American Literature*, Chapel Hill, NC: University of North Carolina Press.

Hesse, Barnor (1999) 'It's your world: Discrepant M/multiculturalisms', in P. Cohen (ed.) *New Ethnicities, Old Racism?*, London: Zed Books.

——(2000) 'Introduction: Un/Settled Multiculturalism', in B. Hesse (ed.) *Un/settled Multiculturalisms: Diasporas, Entanglements, Transruptions*, London: Zed Books.

Herzfeld, Michael (1997) *Cultural Intimacy. Social Poetics in the Nation-State*, New York: Routledge.

Hewitt, Roger (2005) *White Backlash and the Politics of Multiculturalism*, Cambridge: Cambridge University Press.

Hinsliff, Gaby, Rose, David, Burke, Jason and Bright, Martin (2005) 'Terror hunt "to take decades"', *Observer*, 17 July 2005.

Hitchens, Peter (2003) 'When will Britain convert to Islam?', *Mail on Sunday*, 2 November 2003.

Hochschild, Arlie Russel (1983) *The Managed Heart: Commercialization of Human Feeling*, Berkeley: University of California Press.

Holmwood, Leigh and Brook, Stephen (2007) 'Big Brother racism complaints soar', *Media Guardian*, 16 January 2007. Available at: <http://www.guardian.co.uk/race/story/0,1991568,00.html> [last accessed 22 January 2007].

Home Office (2001a) *Community Cohesion. A Report of the Independent Review Team Chaired by Ted Cantle*, London: Home Office.

——(2001b) *Building Cohesive Communities: A Report of the Ministerial Group on Public Order and Community Cohesion*, London: Home Office.

——(2001c) *Secure Borders, Safe Haven. Integration with Diversity in Modern Britain*, London: Stationary Office (CM 5387).

——(2003) *The New And The Old. The Report of the 'Life in the United Kingdom' Advisory Group*. Available at: <http://www.ind.homeoffice.gov.uk/default.asp?pageid = 4271> [last accessed 5 May 2004].

——(2004a) *Strength in Diversity – Towards a Community Cohesion and Race Equality Strategy*, London: Home Office Communication Directorate, June 2004.

——(2004b) *Life in the United Kingdom: A Journey to Citizenship*, London: Stationary Office.

Honneth, Axel (1992) 'Integrity and disrespect. Principles of a conception of morality based on the theory of recognition', *Political Theory*, 20 (2): 187–201.

Howard, Michael (2005) 'Talk about the British dream', *Guardian*, 17 August 2005. Available at: <http://politics.guardian.co.uk/comment/story/0,9115,1550624,00.html> [last accessed 17 August 2005].

Hume, Mick (2000) 'True Brit?', *Times*, 12 October 2000.

Huntington, Samuel (1996) *The Clash of Civilizations and the Remaking of World Order*, New York: Simon & Shuster.

Hussain, Asifa and Miller, William (2006) *Multicultural Nationalism. Islamophobia, Anglophobia, and Devolution*, Oxford: Oxford University Press.

Hutnyk, John (2000) *Critique of Exotica: Music, Politics and the Cultural Industry*, London: Pluto Press.

Hutton, Will (2005) 'We may be vague about who we are, but that could be the most powerful weapon in the war against terror, *Observer*, 31 July 2005. Available at: <http://www.oberver.co.uk> [last accessed 31 July 2005]

Ifekwunigwe, Jayne (1999) *Scattered Belongings: Cultural Paradoxes of Race, Nation and Gender*, London: Routledge.

Ignatiev, Noel (1996) *How the Irish Became White*, New York: Routledge.

Irwin, Jonathan and Hughes, David (2000) 'British is racist, says peer trying to rewrite our history', *Daily Mail*, 10 October 2000.

Johnson, Carol (2002) 'The dilemmas of ethnic privilege: A comparison of constructions of "British", "English" and "Anglo-Celtic" identity in contemporary British and Australian political discourse', *Ethnicities*, 2(2): 163–88.

Johnson, Gordon (2002) 'Gordon Johnson takes a guilt-free look at oddities of imperialism', *Times Higher Education Supplement*, 15 November 2002.

Johnson, Paul (2000) 'In praise of being British', *Daily Mail*, 11 October 2000.

Johnston, Philip (2000) 'Straw wants to rewrite our history', *Telegraph*, 10 October 2000.

——(2004) 'New citizens get a very British welcome', *Telegraph*, 27 February 2004.

Joppke, Christian and Morawska, Ewa (2003) 'Integrating immigrants in liberal nation-states: policies and practices', in C. Joppke and E. Morawska (eds) *Toward Assimilation and Citizenship: Immigrants in Liberal Nation-states*, Basingstoke: Palgrave Macmillan.

Kamboureli, Smaro (1998) 'The technology of ethnicity. Canadian multiculturalism and the language of law', in D. Bennett (ed.) *Multicultural States. Rethinking Difference and Identity*, London & New York: Routledge.

Katz, Jack (1999) *How Emotions Work*, Chicago: University of Chicago Press.

Kelly, Ruth (2006) 'Speech by Ruth Kelly MP at the launch of the new Commission on Integration and Cohesion on 24 August 2006', Department for Communities and Local Government (DCLG) website. Available at: <http://www.communities.gov.uk/index.asp?id = 1502280> [last accessed 25 February 2007].

Kennedy-McFoy, Madeleine (2006) 'Situated citizenships, routed belongings: learning and living French and British citizenship at school', paper presented at the Institute for Women's Studies, Lancaster University, Lancaster, 15 January 2006.

Kepel, Gilles (2005) 'Europe's answer to Londonistan', *Open Democracy*, 24 August 2005. Available at: <http://www.opendemocracy.net/conflict-terrorism/londonistan_2775.jsp#> [last accessed 13 April 2007].

Khanna, Ranjana (2006) 'Post-palliative: Coloniality's affective dissonance', *Post-Colonial Text*, 2(1): 1–20.

King, Colin (2004) *Offside Racism. Playing the White Man*, Oxford: Berg.

Kuhn, Annette (2002) *Family Secrets. Acts of Memory and Imagination*, new edn, London: Verso.

Kundnani, Arun (2001) 'Commentary: From Oldham to Bradford: The violence of the violated', *Race and Class*, 43(2): 105–10.

Laclau, Ernesto and Mouffe, Chantal (1985) *Hegemony and Socialist Strategy. Towards a Radical Democratic Politics*, London: Verso.

Lappin, Tom (2003) 'On TV: A melting pot boiler', *Scotsman*, 27 October 2003.

Laville, Sandra (2000) 'I feel so proud when I see our Union flag', *Daily Telegraph*, 12 October 2000.

Leonard, Mark (2002) 'Living together after 11 September and the rise of the Right', in P. Griffith and M. Leonard (eds) *Reclaiming Britishness*, London: The Foreign Policy Centre.

Lewis, Gail (2004a) '"Do not go gently … ": Terrains of citizenship and landscapes of the personal', in G. Lewis (ed.) *Citizenship, Personal Lives and Social Policy*, Bristol: Policy Press in association with The Open University.

——(2004b) 'Racialising culture is ordinary', in E. B. Silva and T. Bennett (eds) *Contemporary Culture and Everyday Life*, Durham: Sociology Press.

——(2005) 'Welcome to the margins: Diversity, tolerance and policies of exclusion', *Ethnic and Racial Studies*, 28(3): 536–58.

——(2006a) 'Imaginaries of Europe, technologies of gender, economies of power', *European Journal of Women's Studies*, 13(2): 87–102.

——(2006b) 'Journeying toward the nation(al): Cultural difference at the cross-roads of old and new globalisations', *Mobilities*, 1(3): 333–52.

Longley, Edna and Kiberd, Declan (2001) *Multi-Culturalism: The View from the Two Irelands*, Cork: Cork University Press.

Macey, Mary (1999) 'Class, gender and religious influences on changing patterns of Pakistani Muslim male violence in Bradford', *Ethnic and Racial Studies*, 22(5): 845–66.

Manzoor, Sarfraz (2003) 'Isle of white: What's it like to be white – and a minority', *Guardian*, 30 October 2003.

Markley, Robert (2006) *The Far East and the English Imagination, 1600–1730*, Cambridge: Cambridge University Press.

Marks, Laura (2000) *The Skin of the Film: Intercultural Cinema, Embodiment and the Senses*, Durham, NC: Duke University Press.

Marr, Andrew (2000a) *The Day Britain Died*, London: Profile Books.

——(2000b) *The Day Britain Died*, BBC2: 31 January, 1–2 February 2000.

Matthew, Christopher (2003) [no title], *Daily Mail*, 31 October 2003.

Matuštík, Martin J. Beck (1998) 'Ludic, corporate, imperial multiculturalism', in C. Willett (ed.) *Theorizing Multiculturalism. A Guide to the Current Debate*, Oxford: Blackwell.

McClintock, Anne (1995) *Imperial Leather. Race, Gender and Sexuality in the Colonial Context*, New York: Routledge.

McLean, Gareth (2003) 'TV review: It's different for girls', *Guardian*, 31 October 2003.

McSweeney, B. (2000) letter published in the *Sun*, 'Big Issue' Section, 16 October 2000.

Millar, Iain (2003) 'Television', *Independent on Sunday*, 2 November 2003.

Millar, Stuart (2001) 'The way we are: Composite Briton unveiled', *Guardian*, 30 March 2003.

Mirza, Munira, Senthilkumaran, Abi and Ja'far, Zein (2007) *Living Apart Together. British Muslims and the Paradox of Multiculturalism*, London: Policy Exchange.

Mitchell, Katharyne (2004) 'Geographies of identity: Multiculturalism unplugged', *Progress in Human Geography*, 28(5): 641–51.

——(2006) 'Neoliberal governmentality in the European Union: education, train-ing, and technologies of citizenship', *Environment and Planning D: Society and Space*, 24(3): 389–407.

Modood, Tariq (2005) *Multicultural Politics: Racism, Ethnicity and Muslims in Britain*, Edinburgh: Edinburgh University Press.

Modood, Tariq and Werbner, Pnina (eds) (1997) *The Politics of Multiculturalism in the New Europe: Racism, Identity, and Community*, New York: Zed Book.

Modood, Tariq, Zapata-Barrero, Ricard and Triandafyllidou, Anna (eds) (2005) *Multiculturalism, Muslims and Citizenship: a European Approach*, London: Routledge.

Morris, David (1985) 'Gothic Sublimity', *New Literary History*. Available at: <http://www.engl.virginia.edu/enec981/Group/zach.sublime1.html#morris> [last accessed 19 September 2006].

Morris, Nigel and Akbar, Arifa (2004) 'Phil Collins and God Save the Queen: The soundtrack to becoming British', *Independent*, 27 February 2004.

Nayak, Anoop (2006) 'Displaced masculinities: Chavs, youth and class in the post-industrial city', *Sociology*, 40(5): 813–31.

Neal, Sarah (2003) 'The Scarman Report, the Macpherson Report and the media: How newspapers respond to race-centred social policy interventions', *Journal of Social Policy*, 32(1): 55–74.

Noble, Greg (2005) 'The discomfort of strangers: racism, incivility and ontological security in a relaxed and comfortable nation', *Journal of Intercultural Studies*, 26 (1): 107–20.

Nzerem, Keme (2002) 'At school with the shoe bomber', *Guardian*, 28 February 2002.

Office of the Deputy Prime Minister (2005) *Citizen Engagement and Public Services: Why Neighbourhoods Matter*, London: Office of the Deputy Prime Minister.

Oldham Independent Review (2001) *Panel Report: Oldham Independent Review. One Oldham One Future*, Oldham: Oldham City Council.

Ong, Aihwa (2006) *Neoliberalism as Exception. Mutations in Citizenship and Sovereignty*, Durham, NC: Duke University Press.

Ouseley, Sir Herman (2001) *Community Pride not Prejudice. Making Diversity Work in Bradford*. Available at: <http://www.bradford2020.com/pride/report. pdf> [last accessed 5 March 2007].

Owen, Charlie (2001) 'Mixed race in official statistics', in D. Parker and M. Song (eds) *Rethinking 'Mixed Race'*, London: Pluto Press.

Oxford English Reference Dictionary (1995) Oxford: Oxford University Press.

Palmer, Clare (2002) 'Christianity, Englishness and the southern English countryside: A study of the work of H.J. Massingham', *Social & Cultural Geography*, 3 (1): 25–38.

Parker, David (2000) 'The Chinese takeaway and the diasporic habitus: space, time and power geometries', in B. Hesse (ed.) *Un/settled Multiculturalisms. Diasporas, Entanglements, Transruptions*, London: Zed Books.

Parker, David and Miri Song (2001a) (eds) *Rethinking 'Mixed Race'*, London: Pluto.

——(2001b) 'Introduction: Rethinking "Mixed Race"', in D. Parker and M. Song (eds) *Rethinking 'Mixed Race'*, London: Pluto.

Petre, Jonathan (2005) 'Modesty for women', *Daily Telegraph*, 3 March 2005.

Phelan, Peggy (1993) *Unmarked. The Politics of Performance*, London: Routledge.

Phillips, Trevor (n.d.) 'Race Convention: Expert paper to the PM on Community Cohesion'. Available at: <http://www.number10.gov.uk/output/Page10555.asp> [last accessed 23 January 2007].

Povinelli, Elizabeth A. (2002) *The Cunning of Recognition. Indigenous Alterities and the Making of Australian Multiculturalism*, Durham, NC: Duke University Press.

——(2006) *The Empire of Love: Toward a Theory of Intimacy, Genealogy, and Carnality*, Durham, NC: Duke University press.

Probyn, Elspeth (1996) *Outside Belongings*, London: Routledge.

——(2000) *Carnal Appetites. Food Sex Identities*, London: Routledge.

——(2005) *Blush. Faces of Shame*, Minneapolis: University of Minnesota Press.

Puar, Jasbir (1994) 'Writing my way "home". Traveling South Asian bodies and diasporic journeys', *Socialist Review*, 24(4): 75–108.

Puar, Jasbir K. and Rai, Amit S. (2001) 'Monster, terrorist, fag: The war on terrorism and the production of docile patriots', *Social Text*, 20(3): 117–48.

Razack, Sherene H. (2004) 'Imperilled Muslim women, dangerous Muslim men and civilised Europeans: Legal and social responses to forced marriages', *Feminist Legal Studies*, 12: 129–74.

Robson, David (2006) 'Irresistible, the cult that lures young men into martyrdom', *Daily Express*, 12 August 2006.

Roediger, David R. (1991) *The Wages of Whiteness. Race and the Making of the American Working Class*, London: Verso.

——(1994) *Towards the Abolition of Whiteness. Essays on Race, Politics, and Working Class History*, London: Verso.

Rose, Jacqueline (1996) *States of Fantasy*, Oxford: Clarendon Press.

Roy, Anindyo (2005) *Civility and Empire. Literature and Culture in British India, 1822–1922*, Abingdon: Routledge.

Runnymede Trust (The) (1997) *Islamophobia: A Challenge For Us All*, London: Runnymede Trust.

Saharso, Sawitri (2003) 'Culture, tolerance and gender: A contribution from the Netherlands', *European Journal of Women's Studies*, 10(1): 7–28.

Sahgal, Gita (2002) 'Blair's jihad, Blunkett's crusade: The battle for the hearts and minds of Britain's Muslims', *Radical Philosophy*, 112: 2–5.

Said, Edward (1978) *Orientalism*, London, Penguin Books.

Salecl, Renata (2004) *On Anxiety*, London: Routledge.

Sandercock, Leonie (2003) *Cosmopolis II: Mongrel Cities in the Twenty-First Century*, London: Continuum.

Seaton, Matt (2002) 'Parents: My son the fanatic: Are the parents to blame when a child of the west turns Islamist extremist?', *Guardian*, 2 January 2002.

Sedgwick, Eve Kosofsky (2003) *Touching Feeling. Affect, Pedagogy, Performativity*, Durham, NC: Duke University Press.

Sedgwick, Eve Kosofsky and Frank, Adam (eds) (1995) *Shame and its Sisters. A Silvan Tomkins Reader*, Durham, NC: Duke University Press.

Sennett, Richard (1994) *Flesh and Stone. The Body and the City in Western Civilization*, London: Faber and Faber.

Seshadri-Crooks, Kalpana (2000) *Desiring Whiteness*, London: Routledge.

Sharma, Sanjay (2006) *Multicultural Encounters*, Basingstoke: Palgrave Macmillan.

Shaw, P. (2003) letter published in 'Letters Emails', *Daily Star*, 4 November 2003.

Sheller, Mimi (2004) 'Automotive emotions. Feeling the car', *Theory, Culture & Society*, 21(4–5): 221–42.

Shohat, Ella and Stam, Robert (1994) *Unthinking Eurocentrism. Multiculturalism and the Media*, London: Routledge.

Simmel, Georg (1997) 'Metropolis and mental life', in N. Leach (ed.) *Rethinking Architecture: A Reader in Cultural Theory*, New York: Routledge.

Skeggs, Beverly (2004) *Class, Self, Culture*, London: Routledge.

Smithies, Bill and Fiddick, Peter (1969) *Enoch Powell on Immigration*, London: Sphere.

Sollors, Werner (1986) *Beyond Ethnicity, Consent and Descent in American Culture*, Oxford: Oxford University Press.

Sontag, Susan (1977) *On Photography*, New York: Farrar, Straus and Giroux.

Sorkin, Michael (1999) 'Introduction: traffic in democracy', in J. Copjec and M. Sorkin (eds) *Giving Ground. The Politics of Propinquity*, London and New York: Verso.

Sparrow, Andrew (2001) 'I refuse to keep quiet on race, says rebel MP', *Daily Telegraph*, 29 March 2001.

Spickard, Paul (2001) 'The subject is mixed race: The boom in biracial biography', in D. Parker and M. Song (eds) *Rethinking 'Mixed Race'*, London: Pluto.

Stacey, Jackey (2000) 'The global within: The care of the self and the embodiment of health', in S. Franklin, C. Lury and J. Stacey, *Global Nature, Global Culture*, London: Routledge.

Stoetzler, Marcel and Yuval-Davis, Nira (2002) 'Standpoint theory, situated knowledge and the situated imagination', *Feminist Theory*, 3(3): 315–33.

Stoler, Ann Laura (1995) *Race and the Education of Desire*, Durham, NC: Duke University Press.

——(2001) 'Tense and tender ties: The politics of comparison in North American history and (post)colonial studies', *Journal of American History*, 88(3): 829–65.

——(2002) *Carnal Knowledge and Imperial Power: Race and the Intimate in Colonial Rule*, Berkeley: University of California Press.

Straw, Jack (2000) 'Blame the Left, not the British', *Observer*, 15 October 2000.

——(2006) 'I want to unveil my views on an important issue', *Lancashire Telegraph*, East Lancashire blog, 5 October 2006. Available at: <http://www.lancashiretelegraph.co.uk/blog/index.var.488.0.i_want_to_unveil_my_views_on_a-n_important_issue.php#break > [last accessed 6 October 2006].

Sun leading article (2000) 'A disgrace', *Sun*, 12 October 2000.

Taylor, Charles (1994) 'The Politics of recognition', in A. Gutmann (ed.) *Multiculturalism. Examining the Politics of Recognition*, Princeton: Princeton University Press.

Taylor, Matthew (2001) *I'm not racist but* . . . , Channel 4 Television, 22 September 2001.

Taylor, Matthew (2007) 'BNP ballerina dances through protest by anti-racists', *Guardian*, 13 January 2007. Available at: < http://www.guardian.co.uk/farright/story/0,1989460,00.html> [last accessed 13 January 2007].

Thomas, Mandy (2004) 'Sensory displacements: migration and Australian space', plenary address, *Migration, Affect and the Senses conference*, Canberra, Australia, June 2004.

Thompson, Shona (director/producer) (2003) *Cutting Edge: Last White Kids*, Mentorn Productions, Executive Producers: Ros Franey/Alan Hayling, shown on Channel 4, 20 October 2003.

Thomson, Alice (2000) 'Prince Charles "should have married black woman"', *Daily Telegraph*, 17 October 2000.

Thrift, Nigel (2004) 'Intensities of feeling: Towards a spatial politics of affect', *Geografiska Annaler*, 86B(1): 57–78

Tizard, Barbara and Ann Phoenix (2002) *Black, White or Mixed Race? Race and Racism in the Lives of Young People*, revised edn, London: Routledge.

Tolia-Kelly, Divya (2006) 'Affect – an ethnocentric encounter? Exploring the "universalist" imperative of emotional/affectual geographies"', *Area*, 38(2): 213–17.

Tomkins, Silvan (1995) 'Shame-humiliation and contempt-disgust', in E. Kosofsky and A. Frank (eds) *Shame and its Sisters*, Durham, NC: Duke University Press.

Tonkiss, Fran (2003) 'The ethics of indifference: Community and solitude in the city', *International Journal of Cultural Studies*, 6(3): 297–312.

Travis, Alan (2000) 'Be proud to be British, Straw tells left', *Guardian*, 12 October 2000.

Tuori, Salla (2007) 'Cooking nation. Gender equality and multiculturalism as nation-building discourses', *European Journal of Women's Studies*, 14(1): 21–35.

Wald, Priscilla (1995) *Constituting Americans. Cultural Anxiety and Narrative Form*, Durham, NC: Duke University Press.

Ware, Vron (1992) *Beyond the Pale: White Women, Racism and History*, London: Verso.

Weber, Cynthia (1999) *Faking It. U.S. Hegemony in a "Post-phallic" Era*, Minneapolis: University of Minnesota Press.

Weight, Richard (2002) *Patriots. National Identity in Britain 1940–2000*, London: Macmillan.

White, Michael (2000) 'Culture clash at heart of the party', *Guardian*, 5 October 2000.

——(2005) 'PM attacks yob culture and pledges to help bring back respect', *The Guardian*, 13 May 2005. Available at: <http://politics.guardian.co.uk/home-affairs/story/0,1483180,00.html> [last accessed 12 February 2007].

Willcox, Toyah (2002) 'Not in my ravaged paradise', *Sunday Times*, 26 May 2002.

Williams, Raymond (1977) *Marxism and Literature*, Oxford: Oxford University Press.

Wise, Amanda and Chapman, Adam (2005) 'Introduction: Migration, affect and the senses', *Journal of Intercultural Studies*, 26(1): 1–3.

Woodward, Will (2006) 'Blair backs suspension of class assistant in debate over veil', *Guardian*, 18 October 2006.

Wolf, Mark J. P. (2000) 'A brief history of morphing', in V. Sobchack (ed.), *Meta-Morphing. Visual Transformation and the Culture of Quick-Change*, Minneapolis, University of Minnesota Press.

Young, Robert (1995) *Colonial Desire. Hybridity in Theory, Culture and Race*, London: Routledge.

Žižek, Slavoj (1993) *Tarrying with the Negative*, Durham, NC: Duke University Press.

——(1997) 'Multiculturalism, or, the cultural logic of multicultural capital', *New Left Review*, 225: 28–51.

——(1998) 'Love thy neighbor? No, thanks!', in C. Lane (ed.) *The Psychoanalysis of Race*, New York: Columbia University Press.

Zwicky, Arnold (2006) 'More brokeback generalizations', *Language Log*, 9 March 2006. Available at: <http://itre.cis.upenn.edu/~myl/languagelog/archives/2006_03.html>, (March 9 2006) [last accessed 9 April 2007].

Index

eBooks – at www.eBookstore.tandf.co.uk

A library at your fingertips!

eBooks are electronic versions of printed books. You can store them on your PC/laptop or browse them online.

They have advantages for anyone needing rapid access to a wide variety of published, copyright information.

eBooks can help your research by enabling you to bookmark chapters, annotate text and use instant searches to find specific words or phrases. Several eBook files would fit on even a small laptop or PDA.

NEW: Save money by eSubscribing: cheap, online access to any eBook for as long as you need it.

Annual subscription packages

We now offer special low-cost bulk subscriptions to packages of eBooks in certain subject areas. These are available to libraries or to individuals.

For more information please contact webmaster.ebooks@tandf.co.uk

We're continually developing the eBook concept, so keep up to date by visiting the website.

www.eBookstore.tandf.co.uk